P9-CCI-728

THE LITTLE CYANIDE COOKBOOK

DELICIOUS RECIPES RICH IN VITAMIN B17

Second Edition

by June de Spain

Fifth printing: July, 2000
Fourth printing: June, 1978
Third printing: April, 1977
Second printing: May, 1976
First printing: March, 1976

Second edition: July, 2000
First edition: March, 1976

Copyright © 2000 and 1976 by American Media
All rights reserved

Library of Congress Catalog Card Number:
00–134429

International Standard Book Number (ISBN):
0-912986-37-9

Published by American Media
P.O. Box 4646, Westlake Village, California 91359

ADDITIONAL COPIES OF THIS BOOK
may be purchased over the Internet at
www.realityzone.com

For immediate service, order by phone
and charge to your credit card
Call toll-free: (800) 595-6596

ILLUSTRATIONS
BY:
Michele G.
Hellman

Contents

Foreword

This cookbook never would have been written, nor would you likely be interested in reading it, if it were not for the promise it holds as a sort of gourmet's guide to the natural control of cancer. Although my professional background has enabled me to explore the scientific theories behind this promise, nevertheless, I do not consider myself qualified to expound them. For those interested in learning about these theories for themselves, I strongly recommend reading G. Edward Griffin's *World without Cancer; The Story of Vitamin B_{17}*.[1] As for me, suffice it to say simply that I am a firm believer, and that is the reason I have prepared this book.

Dr. Ernst T. Krebs, Jr., the discoverer of vitamin B_{17}, has stated that the best way to treat cancer is *before* it occurs—through good nutrition—not *after*. Once cancer has progressed to the clinically detectable stage, the victim will need far greater quantities of vitamin B_{17} than he likely can obtain from eating normal portions of the foods described in this book. Such persons are urged to consult a physician who is knowledgeable in both vitamin and orthodox therapy so an intelligent choice can be made for the course of treatment.

Upon reading through these recipes, you will discover that I am a purist when it comes to the selection of foods. I do not call for imitation foods or flavorings, baking powder or soda, refined sugar, artificially dyed or flavored gelatins, monosodium glutamate, meat tenderizers, chocolate, refined oils, or a host of other popular products. The simple reason is that I think they are harmful. On the other hand, I do call for certain items that, in all probability, will be substituted in many kitchens because they are difficult to obtain: such things as certified raw milk, sea salt, and organic, fertile eggs. I specify these, nevertheless, as a constant reminder that they are superior to the more common processed substitutes found in most grocery stores. It is my conviction that cancer is due in large measure to poor nutrition. Therefore, I could not in good conscience present recipes in this of all books unless they were above reproach from a nutritional point of view.

Now a word about fats. Not *all* "fats" are good and not *all* fats are bad. In my book I have stressed using the "expeller" pressed oils. These oils are important for health. They are "Cis" fats.

---

1. Published by American Media, Westlake Village, CA.

They have had little processing and are easily metabolized in the human body. "Trans" fats, on the other hand, have been highly heated, bleached, etc., and do harm to us in many ways. When purchasing "Cis" oils, look for those in *colored glass bottles* with the words unrefined and mechanically pressed and expeller pressed. The term "cold pressed" is based on misunderstanding and has absolutely no value as a term denoting oil "quality".

The following oils are good oils if they are untoasted and unhydrogenated:

Unrefined sesame seed oil
Unrefined rice bran oil
Unrefined safflower oil
Unrefined sunflower oil
Unrefined walnut oil
Unrefined soy oil
Unrefined coconut oil
Unrefined olive oil
Unrefined flax seed oil
Unrefined borage oil
Unrefined primrose oil

I am indebted to Patricia Griffin for her unlikely title for this book. Suggested by her first in jest, it soon became obvious that the title has exactly the right mixture of humor and fact to be a perfect choice. And, of course, I am especially grateful to my husband, Lynn, and my son, Forrest, for their willingness to be guinea pigs for these recipes. After many months of sampling, nibbling, and comparing, we all put on a little extra weight that had to be taken off through strenuous exercise and hard restraint. (And I thought that we never could look at another apricot kernel again!) This book would not have been completed without their unselfish and stoic willingness to help.

Those foods shown in bold italics
throughout the following recipes are
sources of vitamin B$_{17}$. See page 189.

Yin Yang Wellness
12131 Westheimer, Unit F
Houston, TX 77077
281-558-8989

Appetizers and Relishes

The appetizer should be just as its name implies, a small morsel of food that stimulates and/or lightly appeases the appetite. It should be small, tasty, and preferably raw. For the sake of good digestion as well as full enjoyment of the dinner, the appetite must not be dulled before the main course but, rather, aroused to zesty anticipation of the delights to come.

A dish of various raw vegetables, placed around a central dipping bowl of seasoned sour cream or yogurt, helps to calm down a ravenous appetite. Bite-sized morsels of raw fruit, such as peaches, plums, or pears, moistened and then coated with ground nuts such as raw almonds or apricot kernels, and arranged on a plate of watercress or alfalfa sprouts, is a pleasant way to start the flow of digestive juices. Raw fruit juices, ice-cold, also whet the appetite, and a small glass of freshly squeezed carrot, tomato, or other vegetable juice is quite piquant to sip while awaiting the main fare.

Apple Chutney

3 C. sliced apples, including ground *seeds*, crushed or grated
⅔ C. *black currants*
1 C. *sorghum cane syrup*
⅓ C. apple cider vinegar
¾ t. sea salt
1½ t. ginger
1½ t. dry mustard
1½ T. curry powder

Mix all the ingredients in saucepan. Bring to a simmer, stirring to blend ingredients. Simmer over low heat for 15 minutes, stirring occasionally. Store in refrigerator. Serve with beef and lamb and with curry dishes. Three cups.

Pineapple Cranberry Relish

2 C. frozen *cranberries*
1 C. dried apricots, soaked in pineapple juice
2 t. *apricot kernels*
½ t. sea salt
1 C. freshly steamed pineapple, chopped
½ C. raw honey

Grind cranberries in blender. Add remaining ingredients, except the pineapple. Fold this in. Chill and serve with meat and poultry. Serves four.

Stuffed Celery

11 stalks celery
3 oz. package of cream cheese
1 T. ground *apricot kernels*
Pinch granulated garlic
1 T. minced organic parsley

Mix last four ingredients together. Stuff celery stalks. Chill and serve.

"Spike"ing Salt

- 1 T. kelp powder
- 3 T. sea salt
- 2 t. curry powder
- 1 t. dried finely ground organic orange peel
- 1 t. dried finely ground organic lemon peel
- 1 t. celery seed
- 2 t. cumin powder
- 1 t. finely ground *apricot kernels*
- 3 t. granulated garlic
- 1 t. tarragon
- 1 t. primary yeast powder
- 1 t. sage
- 1 t. oregano
- 1 t. basil
- 1 t. rosemary
- 1 t. savory
- 1 t. dill weed
- 3 t. granulated onion
- 1 t. mild chili powder or paprika

Crush herbs in palm of hand. Mix all ingredients in bowl. Place in large salt shaker with large holes. Delicious on salads, in soups, mixed with sour cream for dips, etc.

Avocado Butter

Mash one or two avocados depending on their size. Blend with 1-pound raw butter. Blend in juice of 1 lime. Sprinkle ½ t. grated *apricot kernels*. Mince 1 garlic clove. Press into a 1-quart mold and chill overnight. One hour before serving, grind 1 C. raw *filberts*. Roll molded butter in chopped nuts. Place on serving plate and chill until served. Serve with whole-grain crackers and breads.

This dish has a beautiful green color and a delightful flavor.

Apple Bites

- 8 oz. package cream cheese
- 16 *apple seeds*
- 16 raisins
- 1 apple, grated
- 3 T. *apricot kernels*, ground
- Pinch of mace

Mix apple with cream cheese. Place apple seed inside of raisin. Form a small ball of apple and cream cheese with raisins in the middle. Roll in the apricot kernels. Chill several hours.

Indian Curry Slices

3 large red apples, cored and cut into ⅔" slices. Save *apple seeds* for grinding.
4 T. raw butter
1½ t. curry powder
2 T. *sorghum cane syrup*
Pinch sea salt
⅓ C. ground raw coconut
⅓ C. ground raw almonds

Mix butter, curry, and syrup together. Spread on one side of apple slices. Place apples on cookie sheet and place under broiler for about 6 minutes. Remove from oven and sprinkle coconut, almonds, and ground apple seeds over apples. Serve as garnish to meat.

Raisin Sauce for Meat

1 C. heavy, organic beef stock
⅓ C. unsulfured, light raisins
2 T. apple cider vinegar or organic lemon juice
1 organic apple grated
1 t. grated organic lemon rind
10 ground *apple seeds*
1 t. *sorghum cane syrup*
Salt to taste, sea salt

Simmer all ingredients together for about twenty minutes. Serve with meat and curry dishes, etc.

Clam and Cheese Dip

1 can minced clams, well drained
1 large pkg. cream cheese
2½ t. grated onion
2 t. lemon juice, organic
2 t. soy sauce, tamari
2 dashes cayenne pepper
1 T. chopped *watercress*
¼ t. sea salt
1 clove garlic, minced
¼ t. kelp powder
1 T. finely chopped *alfalfa sprouts*
¼ C. clam liquor
Buckwheat and whole-wheat crackers

Add all ingredients carefully except the clam juice and the crackers. Add clam juice, a little at a time, until dip is consistency of whipped cream. Chill. Serve with crackers.

"Spiked" Almonds

2 C. raw almonds (may use pecans or *cashews*)
1 T. *"Spike"ing salt*
1 T. raw butter

Heat butter in skillet gently until it begins to sizzle. Add the almonds and gently warm, do not cook. Sprinkle the seasoned salt on the nuts. Drain on absorbent toweling. Serve as an appetizer.

Clam Dip Non-Dairy

3 eggs, fertile
1¼ C. water
1¼ T. apple cider vinegar
1 t. ground *flax seeds*
1 clove garlic, minced
1 t. sea salt
1 T. miso bean paste or tamari soy sauce
1 t. ground peach *kernels* (op.)
1 C. fresh expeller pressed vegetable oil
1 can clams, well drained

Poach eggs in water and vinegar for three minutes. Pour all into blender. Add all of the remaining ingredients except the clams, blend. Chill and, when firm, stir and fold in the clams. Serve.

Fish and Sea Foods

The average American eats only about ten pounds of fish each year; Scandinavians and Japanese average over 40 pounds each year. Of this 10 pounds, for Americans, fresh and frozen fish account for about 5½ pounds, canned fish for about 4½ pounds. Why don't Americans eat more fish? It's high in nutrition. It's low in cost.

I believe there are several reasons. Truly fresh fish is hard to get unless we catch it ourselves. Frozen fish often is bland and tasteless. Also, few American housewives have learned how to prepare fish so that it is tender and juicy. If the air in the home smells "fishy," the fish has been over-cooked. When fresh and correctly prepared, fish can be outstandingly delicious.

Even more important than it's flavor is it's outstanding nourishment. Fish and seafood have about 18 percent complete, well balanced protein. The flesh is almost completely digestible. It contains only about 20 percent fat and much of this is nutritious, poly-unsaturated fatty-acid compounds. The vitamin content provides A, D, riboflavin and niacin. The mineral content includes high amounts of iodine (mainly ocean fish) magnesium, phosphorus, iron, and copper.

It is also important to note that pollutants are still being dumped into our oceans, and some of them are toxic when consumed in high concentrations. These include the heavy metals mercury and lead. The sea inhabitants ingest these poisons along with their food. The toxins are cumulative. When the levels of intolerance are reached, the animals expire. Unfortunately, when we eat these contaminated fish, their poisons build up in us with the same toxic results. These polluted conditions apparently exist in many areas of the earth today. At the present time, I feel that the safest fish source is in the Icelandic area.

I recommend cold water fish whose oils help keep cholesterol under control and can help lower high blood pressure. These oils are high in the following fish: trout, salmon, mackerel, sardines, and tuna, and are among the highest sources of "Omega-3" fatty acids known today.

I also recommend that you buy the best and freshest fish available, purchased from the safest source. Experiment with new methods of preparation. Serve fish two or three times a week.

When preparing fish, have the heat only moderately hot. Poach or sauté gently. Cook only until the fish "flakes," but is still moist. Slightly "pink" flesh has more flavor and is completely safe to eat. Browned fish is usually over-cooked. Use a sprinkling of paprika instead. To combat blandness, develop a flavorful sauce to serve over the fish.

Seafood Pot Pie

2 T. whole-wheat or
   buckwheat flour
2 T. raw butter
1 C. certified raw milk
   (or home-made "imitation
   cream"*)
2 T. sherry
¼ t. marjoram
¼ t. sage
¼ t. dill weed
1 t. kelp powder
1½ lbs. seafood cut into
   serving pieces
2 potatoes, cooked and cubed
2 carrots, cooked and cubed
6 mushrooms, sliced
1 C. **garbanzo beans**, cooked
 Pastry for top crust made with
   whole-wheat and
   buckwheat flours. (See
   desserts)

Make white sauce by blending
flour and butter in saucepan
over medium heat. When
smooth, add the milk and
sherry. Cook until thick and
smooth. Add the herbs. Place
seafood and vegetables in
casserole dish. Pour sauce on
top and cover with the pastry.
Bake at 375° F. for 45
minutes. Serve with green
salad. Serves four.

* See index

Curried White Fish

2 lbs. fish
2 T. arrowroot powder
6 T. sesame oil
2 t. curry powder
1 C. thinly sliced mushrooms
1 small can **bamboo shoots**
1 organic apple, grated
Seeds from the apple, ground
1 T. lemon juice, organic
1 C. sour cream (or yogurt)
1 t. sea salt
½ t. grated lemon rind, organic
¼ C. minced onion

Coat fish with arrowroot.
Blend the curry powder in the
oil and marinate the fish for
about 1 hour. Brown the
mushrooms, onions, apple,
and apple seeds in a buttered
skillet, over medium heat for
about five minutes. Stir in the
remaining ingredients except
the fish. Place fish and oil in
baking dish. Spoon over sauce
and bake for 30 minutes at
350° F. Baste several times.
Serve with steamed brown
rice. Serves four.

Sautéed Fish with Avocado Sauce

3 lbs. salmon steaks (tuna or
halibut may be substituted)
¾″ thick
2 T. raw butter
½ C. raw butter, melted (for
sauce)
1½ t. sea salt
1 t. prepared brown mustard
1 t. organic lemon juice
1 t. paprika

Place 2 T. butter equally in
two heavy skillets. When it
starts to sizzle, place the fish
in. Make sauce by mixing ½ C.
melted butter, the mustard, the
salt, and lemon juice. Baste
fish frequently with the sauce.
Cook fish gently until flesh
flakes easily. Don't try to
brown it as this dries and
overcooks the fish, sprinkle
with paprika. Serve on large
fish platter decorated with
fresh sprigs of watercress.
Serve avocado sauce on the
side.

Avocado Sauce:

1 ripe avocado
Large handful *watercress*,
rinsed and well drained
½ C. sour cream
1 t. lemon juice, organic
¼ t. sea salt
Dash tabasco
Mix all of the ingredients at
high speed in blender. Chill.
Serve. Serves six.

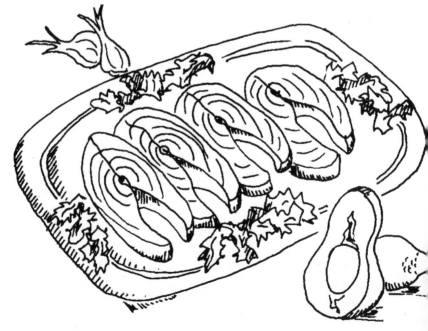

Italian Broiled Shrimp

2 lbs. jumbo shrimp
¼ C. olive oil, imported
¼ C. raw butter
4 cloves garlic, (finely chopped)
Small handful parsley (finely chopped)
¼ C. whole-wheat flour, (or *lima bean flour*)
2 t. ground *peach kernels* or *apricot kernels*
1 C. drawn butter sauce*

Wash and shell shrimp leaving the tails on. Remove veins. Wash again in cold water. Dry, dust with flour. Put olive oil and butter in flat baking dish and heat under low broiler until butter is melted. Place shrimp in baking dish. Broil under low heat for eight minutes. Add garlic and parsley to drawn butter sauce. Pour over shrimp and stir until all shrimp are coated. Return to heat. Broil 2 to 3 minutes. Sprinkle kernels on top. Serve immediately.

*Drawn Butter Sauce

Melt 2 T. butter, add 2 T. whole-wheat flour (or *lima bean flour*), ½ t. freshly ground pepper, 1 t. organic lemon juice, and 1 C. hot water. Bring to a boil stirring constantly and cook for five minutes. Add another 2 T. butter and stir until melted. Serves four.

Poached Fish, Amandine

2 pkgs. frozen Icelandic fish
  (haddock, etc.)
½ C. white wine
½ t. thyme
½ t. sea salt
4 T. raw butter
1 C. fresh raw almonds
1 t. ground *apricot kernels*
1 T. chopped parsley
1 lemon, organic
Sprinkling of paprika

Make court bouillon in heavy skillet: ½ inch water and ¼ C. wine. Add ¼ t. thyme and salt. Place fish in liquid, cover and steam for 8 minutes or until fish flakes. Remove to warm platter. To juices, add butter and ¼ C. wine. Boil down until sauce is rather thick and gelatinous. Pour over fish. Grind almonds in the blender. Mix with apricot kernels and sprinkle over the top. Garnish with parsley, lemon, and paprika. Serve at once.

Fish Fillets with White Grapes

3 T. raw butter, melted
1 lb. fillet, cod, haddock etc.
¼ t. sea salt
¼ C. sherry
2 t. organic lemon juice
Dash cayenne pepper
Pinch grated lemon peel,
  organic
⅔ C. seedless grapes
1 T. golden *currants*
2 t. *apricot* or *peach kernels*
  ground
½ C. ground almonds, raw
Pinch chervil

Place fish in sizzling melted butter in heavy skillet. Brown quickly. Add the wine and cover skillet. Fish should be done in about four to five minutes. Remove to a warm platter. Add lemon juice, peel, grapes, currants and chervil to the skillet and simmer until the grapes are hot. Remove grapes and currants to top of fish. Boil down sauce a little. Spoon over fish. Mix kernels and nuts together and sprinkle on top. Decorate with fresh mint leaves. Serve with tossed green salad. Serves four.

Tuna Almond Crêpes

2 small cans tuna fish, drained
3 T. raw butter
1 C. chopped mushrooms
2 t. *apricot kernels*, ground
⅓ C. chopped onion
⅓ C. chopped celery
⅓ C. chopped black olives
Pinch thyme
Salt and pepper to taste
2 C. Mornay sauce (see sauces)
14 crêpes (see recipe listings in index)
1¼ C. grated raw cheddar cheese

Lightly brown the mushrooms, onions, and celery in the butter. Add the olives, thyme, salt and pepper. Mix in enough sauce to hold filling together. Place two spoonfuls of mixture in the center of each crêpe. Roll up and place in buttered baking dish with the seam down. Fill, roll, and place all crêpes. May make two layers. Cover with the sauce and sprinkle with the cheese. Bake at 375° F. for 15 to 20 minutes. Serve at once with green vegetable and tossed salad. Serves four.

Escalloped Oysters with Lima Beans

1 C. green *lima beans*, cooked
2 pts. eastern oysters, cleaned. Save liquor.
½ C. melted raw butter
2 C. finely crushed whole-wheat crackers
Salt to taste, sea salt
Freshly ground pepper to taste
1 C. cream
Dash nutmeg
½ C. whole-wheat bread crumbs

Butter a 1½ qt. baking dish. Mix 2 C. finely crushed cracker crumbs with ½ C. melted butter. Put crumbs in layers with limas and oysters. Reserve ⅓ C. crumbs for top. Sprinkle each layer with salt and pepper. Mix cream and sand-free oyster liquor together and pour over all. Sprinkle on nutmeg and the top crumbs. Bake at 350° F. for about 35 minutes.

Fish and Mushrooms, Amandine II

1 lb. fish fillets
1 T. raw butter
1 C. sliced mushrooms
1 C. chopped *watercress*
2 t. *apricot kernels*, ground
¼ C. dry sherry
1 T. raw butter
1 t. paprika
1 t. basil

Cook fish gently over medium heat in 1 T. butter, covered. No need to turn fish over. When fish flakes, remove to warm platter. Add sliced mushrooms and cook three minutes. Place on top of the fish. Sprinkle the apricot kernels on top of the mushrooms. Add sherry and more butter to the juices in the pan and boil down to a thick gelatinous gravy. Pour over the fish and sprinkle with the watercress, paprika and crushed basil. Serve at once. Serves four.

Tuna-Buckwheat Casserole

2¼ C. *buckwheat macaroni*
2 C. fresh or canned tuna or other fish
½ C. fresh pineapple
½ C. chopped red bell pepper
⅓ C. chopped unblanched raw almonds
1 T. grated unsweetened coconut
6 slices Swiss cheese (op.)
1½ C. home-made mayonnaise

Cook the macaroni according to instructions. Drain well and mix with remaining ingredients except the cheese and almonds. Place in two-quart casserole or flat baking dish. Lay the cheese on top and bake in 350° F. oven for about 25 minutes. Remove from oven. Sprinkle almonds on top and serve. Serves six.

Seviche, Raw fish recipe from Peru

1½ pounds Iceland fish fillets
4 small hot green chili peppers
2 small hot red chili peppers
7 organic lemons juiced
2 large onions, thinly sliced
Salt to taste, sea salt
Pepper to taste
1 clove garlic, minced
1 small handful minced
   parsley
1 t. *flax seeds*
½ C. mushrooms, thinly sliced

Slice raw fish into thin strips. Remove seeds of chilies and save for later. Cut chilies into thin strips. Combine with remaining ingredients. Chill for 24 hours. Sprinkle with parsley and serve. Serves four.

Baked Fish Fillets

1 lb. fish fillets
1 C. grated raw cheddar
   cheese
3 organic tomatoes, diced
1 T. minced parsley
2 T. grated onion
1½ T. raw butter
Freshly ground black pepper
2 t. ground *apricot kernels*
Salt to taste, sea salt

Place cleaned and dried fish on cookie sheet. Sprinkle with salt and pepper, grated onion, and butter. Place diced tomatoes on top. Bake at 350° F. until fish flakes. Medium thick fish take about 20 minutes. Sprinkle with cheese. Return to oven until cheese is melted. Sprinkle with parsley and grated apricot kernels. Serve at once. Serves four.

Pickled Herring

1 lb. salted herring
Water to cover
1 medium onion, thinly sliced
1 T. whole allspice
Pepper to taste
Salt to taste, sea salt
2 T. *sorghum cane syrup*
Apple cider vinegar to cover

Soak the salted herring for three days; changing the water twice a day. Cut the fish up into pieces. Layer in a heavy crock with thinly sliced onions. Sprinkle with whole allspice, salt and pepper. Mix the syrup and vinegar and pour over the fish. Refrigerate for two days. Serve with sour cream. Serves four.

Seafood Custard

1 lb. seafood (lobster, clams, crab, whitefish, etc.)
4 eggs
⅓ C. melted raw butter
1 t. kelp
1 t. dill weed
1 T. dried mustard
1 t. sea salt
1 C. raw milk
1 C. rich cream
3 t. minced bell pepper
½ C. whole-wheat cracker crumbs
2 T. raw butter
2 t. ground *apricot kernels*

Halibut Baked in Yogurt

1 lb. fish fillets, halibut or other white fish
1 C. yogurt
1 T. raw butter
1 t. kelp powder
1 t. dill weed
Pinch dry mustard
Pinch ginger
Pinch basil
Pinch paprika
½ C. *macadamia nuts*, chopped

Place fish in flat baking dish. Mix herbs with yogurt. Spread over the fish. Sprinkle the top with paprika. Bake at 350° F. until fish flakes. Sprinkle with macadamia nuts. Serve at once. Serves four.

Place the fish in a buttered baking dish. Mix the remaining ingredients, except the crumbs, bell pepper, and the last butter in the blender and pour over the fish. Add the peppers. Sprinkle the crumbs and dots of butter over the top. Bake at 325° F. for about 50 minutes or until custard is well set. Serve with green peas and millet bread. Serves four.

Oriental Sweet and Sour Shrimp

2 C. shrimp, shelled and
  de-veined
3 T. sesame oil
3 large green bell peppers, cut
  in squares
1 large green onion, chopped
  finely
2 chilies, chopped, mild
5 T. honey
1 t. sea salt
3 T. water
3 T. tomato paste
3 T. apple cider vinegar
1 T. soy sauce, tamari
1 T. arrowroot
2 t. **apricot kernels**, ground

Slice shrimp in half lengthwise. Heat oil in skillet. Add the shrimp and chilies. Sauté until the shrimp turns pink. Add the green peppers, onion, honey, salt, 2 T. water, tomato paste, and vinegar. When mixture starts to simmer, add the arrowroot and 1 T. water, mixed. Add the soy sauce and stir until clear and thickened. Serve over long grain brown rice. Sprinkle the apricot kernels on top.

Meat

"Red" meat is becoming increasingly expensive. And, unfortunately, much of the commercial meat commonly available is questionable, to say the least, as to its real value as a source of human nutrition. Many people are opposed to current butchering practices in the United States. Many others are opposed to the artificial hormone injections which could be harmful to the consumer. Some members of the medical profession feel that meat competes with certain pancreatic enzymes believed to be effective in the natural control of cancer.

These "red" meats are not required in the human diet if the essential amino acids are supplied from other sources. However, except for special medical diets, a certain amount of these meats can be beneficial. Meat is high in amino acids. Having the essential "basic eight," it is a complete protein food. The flesh and organs of freshly killed and quickly eaten wild animals would be best. They have all of the essential food elements for human survival. Wild animals feed on plants high in nitrilosides, such as vetch and Johnson grass. Their blood is rich in B_{17}, iron, iodine, zinc and other minerals. There is very little fat. Whatever fat there is, is high in vitamin A.

Civilized man, on the other hand, has developed the habit of "aging" meat for ten to fifteen days. The final product is more tender but devoid of most of the original vitamins and some of the minerals.

I recommend only "naturally grown" beef, veal, lamb and as much wild meat as can be obtained, such as goat, deer, bear and so forth. "Domestic" pork is so high in hard fat and insecticide residues that it is not recommended. Neither is the sausage or ham derived from it. These are filled with dye, nitrates, nitrites, great quantities of salt, and many other chemicals of doubtful effect on the human body.

When the portion of meat is a tender cut, cook it as little as possible. When a tougher cut is selected, cook it gently over low heat for a longer period. Never forget that a living creature gave up it's life for the continuation of your life, and cremation should not be its finale.

Cantonese Chow Mein

4 C. almond noodles, home-made, cooked (see cereals)

½ C. peapods*, "string," and slice the big ones in half

1 onion, sliced thinly

2 celery stalks, sliced diagonally

1 C. mushrooms, sliced thinly

2 C. *mung bean sprouts* (leave green skins on)

1 lb. lean beef or chicken, frozen and when partially thawed, sliced thinly

1 t. sea salt

1 t. *sorghum cane syrup*

½ C. raw almonds, cracked

2 T. soy sauce, tamari

2 t. arrowroot

3 T. sesame oil

1 green onion, chopped

2 T. water or stock

2 t. *apricot kernels*, ground

1 bell pepper, sliced diagonally

Mix the meat with the arrowroot, 2 T. soy sauce, salt, syrup, and 1 T. oil. Set aside. Sauté the noodles until lightly brown. Set aside on warm platter. Cook the meat in a medium hot skillet until brown. Drain and set aside. Place vegetables in skillet, add the water and stir to heat. Cover and steam for five minutes. Stir in the meat. Make a hollow in the center of the skillet and pour the arrowroot and soy sauce mixture in the center. Stir until sauce is thickened. Pour over the noodles. Sprinkle the top with the almonds, apricot kernels, and chopped green onion. Serve at once. Serves four.

*Also called Chinese peas or snow peas

Beef and Bean Ragoût

½ calf heart cut into thin strips or 2 lbs. organic stewing beef
1 onion
1 carrot
1 parsnip
½ C. dry wine
4 T. raw butter
4 T. whole-wheat flour
1 T. *sorghum cane syrup*
3 T. browned onions
2 T. parsley, chopped
2 T. organic lemon juice and a little rind
2 C. cooked *fava beans* (or *lima* or *"shell" beans*)
2 T. chopped capers
2 T. chopped anchovies
Salt and pepper to taste, sea salt
¾ C. thick cream
½ C. Parmesan cheese

Cook meat in large kettle with onion, carrot, wine, and parsnip until tender. Drain and place meat on warm platter. Save the stock. Place the beans on top of the meat. Make a cream gravy by blending the butter and flour together in saucepan over medium heat until smooth. Add stock and stir until thick and smooth. Add the remaining ingredients and pour over the meat and beans. Sprinkle the top with cheese and serve. Serves six.

Beef Ragoût

2 lbs. organic beef, lean, cubed
2 T. raw butter
1 onion, chopped
1 clove garlic, minced
2 large tomatoes, cut into sixths
2 bell peppers, sliced thinly
½ lb. mushrooms, sliced thinly
2 C. beef stock
1 C. cooked *fava beans*

Brown the beef and onion in the butter. Add the stock and garlic and cook, covered for 2 hours. Ten minutes before serving, add the beans, tomatoes, mushrooms, and peppers. Cook covered. Serve over home-made noodles. (See cereals) Serves four.

Beef Stroganoff

2 lbs. very thinly sliced organic
    round steak in strips
4 T. raw butter (2 T. may be oil)
½ C. **buckwheat flour** or **lima
    bean flour**
1 C. yogurt or sour cream
1 clove garlic, minced
1 t. sea salt
Freshly ground pepper to taste
½ lb. sliced mushrooms (op.)

Mix the flour, salt, and pepper
together and dust the meat. Heat
the butter to sizzle and add the
meat, a few strips at a time. Try
not to let strips touch each other.
This "stews" the meat and it
does not brown quickly. Turn
meat, being careful not to
over-cook. Remove slightly rare
meat to warm platter and
continue cooking until all meat
is done. A little more fat may be
needed. Brown the mushrooms
for only a minute and place on
top of the meat. Add garlic and
yogurt to skillet. Heat gently,
stirring and scraping brown
crust from skillet. Do not boil.
Salt to taste and spoon over the
meat. Serve at once. Serves
four.

Almond Steak

1½ lbs. top sirloin steak,
    organic
4 T. almonds, raw, freshly
    ground in blender
1 t. **apricot kernels**, ground
1 T. olive oil or raw butter
Salt to taste, sea salt
¼ C. brandy or apple juice
4 T. **watercress**, chopped

One hour before cooking,
press ground almonds into
steak. Let stand at room
temperature for one hour. Heat
fat in heavy frying pan. Pan
broil steak to desired
doneness. Season to taste with
salt and place on warm platter.
Sprinkle top with chopped
watercress. Add kernels to the
juices in the skillet. Add the
brandy and flame. Heat until
slightly thickened. Spoon over
steak and serve. Serves two.

Blanquette of Veal

2 lbs. breast or shoulder of veal
2 C. water
½ C. white wine
1 t. sea salt
1 onion
1 carrot, cut up
2 T. whole-wheat flour or *lima bean flour*
2 T. raw butter
9 small pearl onions
9 mushrooms, chopped
Pinch thyme
Pinch clove
2 fertile egg yolks, beaten
4 oz. raw cream
Pinch nutmeg
⅛ t. bay leaf, crushed
½ C. sherry
1½ C. chicken stock or veal stock
1 C. cooked green *lima beans*, heated

Bone and cube the veal. Cook for 1½ hours in water and wine. Twenty-five minutes before veal is done put carrot and onions in with veal and cook. In saucepan, brown the mushrooms in the butter. Stir in the flour and, when smooth, add the sherry and chicken stock. Stir a little sauce into the egg yolks, then stir egg yolks into sauce. Add spices. Do not boil after egg yolks have been added. Stir in the cream and salt to taste. Drain the veal and vegetables. Place on large warm platter. Put limas on top and pour white sauce over all. Serve at once.

Lamb Curry

2½ lb. boned lamb, cubed
1 T. raw butter
1 T. minced onion
1 T. curry powder
Pinch of the following: basil, thyme, rosemary, sage
1 clove garlic, minced
1 t. sea salt
1 grind of fresh pepper
1½ C. stock or water
1 t. grated organic lemon peel
1½ C. *mung bean sprouts*
2½ t. arrowroot

Brown the lamb and onions in the butter. Add the remaining ingredients except the arrowroot. Simmer, covered for about two hours. When lamb is tender, remove it to a warm platter. Stir the arrowroot into the juices in the pan. Stir until sauce has thickened. Pour over lamb. Serve in bowls over hot buttered brown rice. Serve chutney, raisins, coconut, etc. on the side. Serves four.

French-Italian Spaghetti Sauce with Buckwheat Spaghetti

Spaghetti:
1 lb. *buckwheat spaghetti*
1 T. olive oil (or other)
2 qts. water for cooking
    spaghetti
1 T. sea salt

Cook spaghetti in large pot of boiling water to which salt and oil have been added. When the spaghetti is tender, but not mushy, drain and toss with 2 T. butter or olive oil.

Sauce:
2 small onions, finely chopped
¼ C. olive oil
3 garlic cloves, minced
1 large can tomato purée
1 small can tomato paste
2 C. beef stock or water
¼ T. sage
¼ T. marjoram
¼ T. rosemary
¼ T. thyme
1 C. chicken livers, cut into
    tiny pieces (op.)
½ lb. fresh mushrooms, sliced
    thinly

Brown liver, onions, garlic and mushrooms in oil. Add herbs, stock and tomato. Cook gently, covered for about two hours. Serve over spaghetti. Sprinkle grated Parmesan cheese on top. Hot chili seeds on the side, if desired.

Lamb Shanks in Fruit and Wine

4 lamb shanks
2 T. **buckwheat flour**
¾ C. unsulfured raisins (or dried **black currants**)
¾ C. unsulfured prunes and their ground **kernels**
¾ C. unsulfured apricots and their ground **kernels**
¾ C. dry wine
½ C. **sorghum cane syrup**
4 T. fresh organic lemon juice
½ t. cinnamon
½ t. allspice
½ t. sea salt

Dust lamb shanks in flour and salt. Place in baking pan, cover and bake for 1 hour and 40 minutes at 350° F. While the lamb is roasting make a sauce with the remaining ingredients. Heat gently and cook for about 10 minutes. During the last 30 minutes of roasting, drain the excess fat from the lamb and pour sauce on top. Cover and bake at 375° F. Serve with fresh spinach salad or Tabouli salad. Serves four.

Calves Liver and Onions

1 lb. calves liver, cut into bite-sized pieces
2 T. raw butter
1½ C. whole-wheat flour
2 t. **apricot kernels**, ground
1 t. sea salt
Freshly ground pepper
2 medium sized onions, chopped
2 C. cooked potatoes, cubed
2 T. raw butter
½ C. chopped parsley

Place flour, salt, pepper and apricot kernels in brown paper bag. Shake to mix. Add liver and shake until the liver is thoroughly coated. Brown liver and cook through. Set aside. Brown onions in 2 T. butter, add and lightly brown the potatoes. Add the liver and parsley and serve. Serves four.

Teriyaki Beef

2 lbs. sirloin steak, thinly
    sliced*
2 t. freshly grated ginger
1 clove garlic, minced
1 onion, chopped
⅓ C. soy sauce, tamari
¼ C. *sorghum cane syrup*
¼ C. sherry
2 t. *apricot kernels*, ground

Mix all ingredients together
except the meat. Stir and cook
over low heat until thoroughly
mixed. Cool and pour over the
steak slices. Marinate for
several hours. Broil three
minutes on each side. Best to
broil over charcoal. Serves
four.

This marinade is also very
good for ribs and chicken.

 *To slice the beef very thinly,
freeze it and then partially
thaw it. Slice across the grain
with a sharp knife.

Beef Carbonade (Pot Roast Belgian Style)

3 lbs. chuck, sliced ½″ thick,
    organic
2 T. butter
¼ C. consommé
1 t. *buckwheat flour*
½ t. sea salt
Freshly ground pepper to taste
1 bay leaf
6 medium sized onions,
    chopped
1 t. *sorghum cane syrup*
1 C. beer, (imported Dutch is
    good)

Heat butter in heavy skillet.
Dredge the meat with the
flour, salt and pepper. Add the
meat to the butter and brown
on both sides. Remove meat
and set aside. Add onions to
the pan and brown gently. Stir
in the consommé and beer.
Bring to simmer and return the
meat to the pan. Add the
seasonings. Cover and simmer
three hours or until meat is
tender. Serve with noodles or
boiled potatoes.

Sweetbreads in Almond Sauce

2 prs. sweetbreads (or brains), blanched*
4½ T. raw butter
½ C. raw almonds, ground
1 t. **bitter almonds** or **apricot kernels**, ground
2 t. arrowroot
6 fresh mushrooms, minced
¼ t. crushed bay leaf
1 vegetable bouillon cube
⅓ C. sweetbread stock
⅓ C. dry white wine
1½ t. tomato paste

Brown the cooked, blanched sweetbreads and mushrooms in the butter. Remove and set aside. Mix arrowroot in hot butter until smooth. Add wine and stock and stir until thick; blend in other ingredients and pour over sweetbreads. Serve on toast points. Green peas are usually served with sweetbreads. Serves four.

*Blanching: Wash sweetbreads and soak in cold water for 40 minutes, changing water three times. Drain, cover with cold water. Add 1 T. white wine vinegar and 1 t. salt. Bring to a boil, simmer, covered for 15 minutes, drain and cover with ice water. When cool enough to handle, remove membrane and tubes. Cut into cubes.

Armenian Moussaka

2 C. cooked **lentils**, drained
1 lb. ground beef
1 eggplant, diced
3 T. olive oil, may need a little more
1 onion chopped
1 clove garlic, minced
1 small can tomato paste
1½ C. water (lentil water good)
Salt and pepper to taste, sea salt
1 C. diced raw cheese
½ C. Parmesan cheese

Lightly brown the onion, garlic, eggplant and beef in olive oil in skillet. Add water and tomato paste. Slightly cook down. Place beans in bottom of baking dish. Layer cheese and beef mixture on top. Sprinkle Parmesan cheese on top. Bake at 350° F. until hot and bubbly and the cheese on top has browned. This will be about 20 to 25 minutes. Serve at once with green salad. Serves four.

Salisbury Steaks in Sour Cream

1½ lbs. stewing beef, organic, freshly ground
4 T. raw butter
1 onion, chopped finely
1 egg, fertile
½ C. *macadamias*, chopped
1 t. nutmeg
1 t. tarragon
1½ t. sea salt
Freshly ground black pepper
½ C. *buckwheat flour*
½ C. beef stock or bouillon
1 C. sour cream

Brown onions lightly in 2 T. butter. Mix hamburger with egg, nuts, herbs, salt, pepper and browned onions. Form into six patties. Dredge in the flour and brown the patties. Cook gently for about six minutes or until still slightly pink inside. Remove to warm platter. Add stock and cream to drippings. Heat gently, scraping and mixing in the drippings. Spoon over meat and serve. Serves six.

Beef Bourguignonne (Beef in Burgundy)

3 lbs. stewing beef, cubed
2 T. raw butter
2 C. burgundy wine
4 T. *buckwheat flour*
½ C. consommé
24 pearl onions
1 C. sliced mushrooms
1 bay leaf
Pinch thyme
4 sprigs *watercress* (save for platter)
1 large onion, chopped
Handful parsley, chopped
1 clove garlic, minced
1 carrot, chopped
1 t. *sorghum cane syrup*

Brown the meat in the butter. Sprinkle the flour over the meat and cook for 3 minutes. Stir in consommé, vegetables, wine and seasonings. Cook about 45 minutes. Remove vegetables and replace with mushrooms and onions. Resume cooking until meat is tender. Skim off excess fat and season to taste. Serve with home-made noodles. (See cereals.)

Danish Liverwurst

1 lb. liver, cut up
1 C. cream
½ C. *buckwheat flour*
3 T. raw butter
1 T. sea salt
⅛ t. celery salt
1 t. pepper
1 fertile egg
1 T. onion, chopped

Veal Scallopini

2 T. *buckwheat flour*
1 t. sea salt
¼ t. freshly ground pepper
2 lbs. unpounded veal cutlets
½ C. chopped *watercress*
3 T. raw butter
1 bouillon cube, salt-free
    Swiss make
4 T. Marsala wine

Blend egg and cream in blender. Add rest of ingredients and blend. Strain to remove gristle. Place in a loaf pan in a pan of water. Bake 1 to 1¼ hours at 350° F. There will be a golden brown crust on top. Serves six.

Mix flour, salt and pepper and set aside. Pound the cutlets until very thin. Coat the veal in the flour mixture. Place butter in skillet and heat to sizzle. Sauté the veal gently for 5 minutes on each side over medium heat. Dissolve the bouillon cube in 3 T. hot water. Remove the veal to a warm platter. Add bouillon to juices in the pan. Stir in the wine and boil the sauce down to a thin gelatinous gravy. Spoon over the veal. Sprinkle the top with chopped watercress. Serve. Serves six.

Lima-Bean Hamburger Loaf

1 C. cooked *lima bean* purée
1 C. freshly ground hamburger
½ C. raw milk
2 organic fertile eggs
1 t. sea salt
1 grind of fresh black pepper
½ C. dry rolled oats
1 clove garlic, minced
1 onion, chopped
½ C. unroasted pecans or
    cashews

Soak dried lima beans overnight. Drain (save water for plants). Cook until tender. Blend until puréed. Mix and place in loaf. Decorate top with a row of raw pecan halves. Serves four.

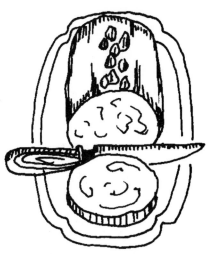

Almond Beef Hash

4 C. diced leftover beef
4 C. diced cooked potatoes
3 T. raw butter
1 onion, diced
⅓ C. dry wine
1 t. *sorghum cane syrup*
3 T. miso soy bean paste or
    soy sauce, tamari
3 T. tomato purée or paste
⅔ C. raw cream
1 t. basil
Dash paprika
2 t. *apricot kernels*, ground

Brown the meat, onions and potatoes in the butter. Pour the wine over the meat mixture. Mix the remainder of the ingredients, except the kernels, together. Place meat mixture in casserole and pour sauce on top. Bake at 350° F. for 15 minutes. Sprinkle kernels on top and serve. Serves four.

Calves Liver with Raw Cashews

1 lb. calves liver, sliced thinly
5 T. raw butter
6 T. garlic wine vinegar
1 T. *sorghum cane syrup*
1 t. sea salt
½ C. ground *cashews*, raw
½ C. grated Parmesan cheese

Brown liver in butter. Add vinegar and syrup and cook
through. Mix salt, and Parmesan cheese. Sprinkle over the liver
and place under the broiler for a few minutes to brown.
Sprinkle on the cashews. Serve at once. Serves four.

Poultry

Poultry is rich in all the essential amino acids and it is relatively inexpensive. There are well over one thousand ways to serve poultry. Buy only that poultry which is raised on the ground and fed natural grains free of pesticides, hormones and antibiotics. Cook with moderate to low heat, being very careful not to over-cook. Save any gravy or stock for soups and sauces. Boil the bones several hours with a little wine or apple cider vinegar for an exceptionally nutritious soup, rich in minerals.

Oriental Chicken

4 boned and skinned whole chicken breasts
1 medium pineapple, cut into small chunks
¼ C. soy sauce, tamari
2 T. raw butter
2 T. honey or *sorghum cane syrup*
2 T. sherry
1½ t. sea salt
2 cloves minced garlic
1 lemon, thinly sliced
½ C. chopped *macadamia nuts*
½ C. unsweetened coconut
1 T. arrowroot dissolved in 3 T. cold water
1 onion, thinly sliced lengthwise
1 bell pepper, thinly sliced lengthwise
4 C. cooked long grain brown rice

Remove the skin and the bones from the chicken. Boil scraps to make a stock. Cut chicken into small chunks. Melt the butter in large, heavy skillet. When it's sizzling, gently brown the chicken on both sides. Add the honey, sherry, soy sauce and cover.

Simmer for 25 minutes. Add onion, pineapple, and pepper. Re-cover and steam 4 minutes. Add nuts, stir, and remove contents of skillet to a warm platter, leaving the drippings in the skillet. Add the dissolved arrowroot. Stir over medium heat until the sauce is thick and clear. Pour over the chicken. Decorate with lemon slices. Top with coconut and serve with rice on the side.

Variation: If sweet and sour sauce is preferred, add ¼ C. apple cider vinegar and ¼ C. tomato purée to the juices in the skillet. Add 2 T. arrowroot dissolved in 6 T. water or cold stock. Serves four.

Rex's Chicken Salad with Sour Cream

4 whole chicken breasts
1 bell pepper, chopped, including seeds
2½ T. organic lemon juice
1 C. sour cream (or yogurt)
Freshly ground black pepper to taste
Salt to taste, sea salt
Pinch ground clove
2½ t. chopped chives
¼ t. oregano
¼ t. rosemary
¼ t. sweet basil
¼ t. *apricot kernels*, grated

Remove skin and bone from chicken breasts. Sauté or steam meat until just done (10 to 15 minutes). Cut into small cubes and mix with remaining ingredients. Chill for several hours. Serve on nests of chopped lettuce, raw spinach leaves, and alfalfa sprouts. Decorate with tomato wedges, fresh mint leaves, sprigs of watercress, and fresh lemon wedges.

Chicken Supreme

3 whole chicken breasts
⅓ C. raw butter
⅓ C. dry wine or apple juice
⅓ C. chicken stock or water
1¼ C. raw cream
Salt and pepper to taste
1 T. organic lemon juice
Handful chopped mint
Handful *watercress*
½ C. raw *cashews*, chopped

Remove, or have butcher remove, the breast meat from the chickens. Remove the skin. Boil breast bones and skin for twenty-five minutes for stock. Sauté the breasts gently for about seven minutes. Don't over-cook or they will be tough. Remove them to a warm platter. Add the wine and stock to the drippings and simmer down to a thick sauce. Add the lemon juice and stir in. Add the cream and mint and just heat through. Spoon over the chicken. Sprinkle the nuts on top. Serve at once, decorated with the watercress. Serves four.

Oven "Fried" Chicken

2 small friers, cut up (skin removed for special diets)
1½ C. whole-wheat flour (*buckwheat flour* for special diets)
1 t. sea salt
1 T. sage
3 T. ground *apricot kernels*

Rinse chickens and pat dry. Put rest of the ingredients in a paper bag. Place chicken in bag and shake until completely coated. Place chicken on oiled cookie sheet. Bake in 350° F. oven for one hour, turning chicken once. A little extra breading may be sprinkled on the chicken before turning and after. Serves four.

Sherried Chicken with Artichokes

3 lb. frying chicken, cut into parts
Sea salt, pepper, and paprika to taste
5 T. raw butter
2 C. artichoke hearts
½ lb. fresh mushrooms, sliced
¼ C. finely minced onion
2 T. *buckwheat flour*
¼ C. chicken stock
¼ C. sherry
½ t. rosemary

Sprinkle the chicken with salt, pepper, and paprika to taste. Brown the pieces in the butter in heavy skillet. Transfer the chicken to an oven casserole dish alternating with the artichokes. Add the mushrooms and onions to the drippings in the pan and sauté for five minutes. Sprinkle the flour over and stir in. Pour over the chicken. Cover the casserole dish and bake at 375° F. for about 50 minutes. Serve at once with fresh tossed salad. Serves four.

Avocado Chicken Tostada

4 corn tortillas, stone-ground
6 T. sesame oil
2 C. home-made chili con carne with small white *lima beans*, thick and hot
6 C. shredded iceberg lettuce
1 C. home-made chili sauce (mild)
1 C. Parmesan cheese
12 slices of chicken, cooked and chilled, skinned
2 avocados, peeled and sliced lengthwise
Garnish with radishes, tomato wedges, green onions, olives, etc.

Fry the tortillas, one at a time, in the hot oil until crisp and brown. Drain and place one on each serving plate. Spoon the hot chili over the top of each tortilla. Toss shredded lettuce with about half of the home-made chili sauce. Pile the lettuce in a stack over the hot chili. Take half the cheese and sprinkle over each serving. Arrange the chicken and avocado slices on top of the center stacks of lettuce. Sprinkle with remaining chili sauce, then with remaining cheese. Garnish each serving with radishes, tomato wedges, green onions, and olives. Serves four.

Miso* Chicken

1 chicken, cut up
1 fertile egg
1 T. miso bean paste
1 T. sea salt
Freshly ground pepper to taste
1 clove garlic, minced
½ C. *buckwheat flour* or whole-wheat flour
1 C. finely ground dry breadcrumbs (may be from wheat-free bread)

Mix the miso, egg, salt, and pepper. Dip the pieces of chicken into the mixture. Coat with the flour and breadcrumbs. Fry. Serves four.

*Miso is an aged soy bean paste that has the color and flavor similar to soy sauce but stronger.

Chicken and Buckwheat Amandine in Ramekins

4 oz. cooked *buckwheat spaghetti*

2 C. cooked chicken (fish may be substituted)

2 T. whole-wheat flour (or *buckwheat flour*)

2 T. raw butter (or oil)

1 C. cream (or home-made "imitation cream")

1 C. chicken broth

1 C. fresh green peas, lightly cooked

1¼ C. raw cheddar cheese (op.)

½ C. unblanched raw almonds, cracked

1 t. *apricot kernels*, ground

½ t. sea salt

1½ t. soy sauce, tamari

4 sprigs *watercress*

Make cream sauce by melting butter in saucepan. Add flour and blend to a paste. Add broth. Stir until thick and smooth. Turn heat down, add cheese and stir until melted. Add soy sauce and cream. Do not reboil.

Assemble 4 ramekins by first dividing spaghetti into four portions and placing it in the bottom of the ramekins. Next, place the chicken on top of the spaghetti. The peas go on top of this. Spoon the cheese sauce over all. Bake in 350° F. oven until brown and bubbly for about 20 minutes. Sprinkle the almonds and ground kernels on top and add a sprig of watercress. Serve with raw vegetable salad. Serves four.

Chicken a la Crème, Wheat-Free

3 lb. frying chicken, cut up
6 T. **buckwheat flour** or **lima bean flour**
½ t. sea salt
¼ t. pepper
2 C. raw cream*
4 T. hot raw milk*

Mix the flour with the salt and pepper. Coat the chicken pieces with mixture. Place in a shallow baking dish. Pour the cream on top and bake for about 2 hours in a 325° F. oven, turning the pieces over after one hour. Place the chicken on a platter. Thin the gravy down, if desired, with a little milk and pour over the chicken. Serves four.

Variation: Raw almonds or cashews are very good baked with this.

*Home-made "Imitation Cream" may be used in place of the cream, and yogurt or water may be used in place of the milk in this recipe to make more "Dairy-free."

Walnut Chicken

1 lb. breast of chicken, skin and bone-free
½ C. celery, sliced
1 large onion, sliced
4 oz. can water chestnuts, sliced
¼ t. sea salt
1 T. arrowroot
3 T. soy sauce, tamari
2 T. dry white wine or apple juice
1 C. walnuts, raw
8 T. oil
½ C. **bamboo shoots**, cubed
Pinch grated ginger
5 mushrooms, sliced

Cut the chicken into 1½" pieces. Dredge in the arrowroot and salt, then do the same with the soy sauce and wine. Set aside. Gently heat the walnuts in 3 T. of the oil for about two minutes. Remove from the skillet. Add the remainder of the oil and when it's hot and sizzling, but not smoking, cook the chicken until golden brown. Remove. Add vegetables and steam for four minutes. Add the meat. Add the walnuts and serve. Serves four.

Chicken Marengo

4 T. raw butter
4 T. *buckwheat flour*
1 t. sea salt
Freshly ground pepper to taste
3 chicken breasts, skin
   removed
3 garlic cloves, minced
½ lb. mushrooms, sliced
4 tomatoes, segmented
1 C. white wine
½ C. brandy
¼ t. thyme
Small handful parsley, minced
1 bay leaf

Mix the flour, salt, and pepper.
Sprinkle over the chicken
pieces. Sauté in butter that is
sizzling in the skillet. Brown
for a few minutes on each
side. Place in heavy oven-
proof casserole, pouring butter
over the top. Add the brandy,
wine, bay leaf, thyme, and
garlic. Cover and cook over
medium heat for about
forty-five minutes. During the
last ten minutes add the
tomatoes, mushrooms and
parsley. Serve over brown
and/or wild rice. Serves six.

Flambé Chicken with Shallots

3 whole chicken breasts, bone
   and skin removed
6 T. raw butter
3 shallots, chopped finely
¼ C. hot brandy
2 T. hot gin
2 t. tarragon
¼ C. cream (or home-made
   "imitation cream")
Handful of *watercress*,
   chopped

Melt 4 T. butter in heavy
skillet. When it's sizzling
gently, add the chicken and
brown lightly for about five
minutes on each side. Add the
shallots and cook two or three
more minutes until the chicken
is just done. Add the brandy
and gin and light the sauce
with a match. The alcohol will
flame off. Add 2 T. of butter
and the cream. Heat through
but do not boil as the cream
will curdle. Serve at once on
warm platter with the sauce
spooned on top, and the
watercress sprinkled over all.
Serves six.

Roast Almond Duck

1 duck, 5 lbs. washed and
    blotted dry
1 C. almonds, raw, cracked
3 t. *apricot kernels*, ground
1 C. sweet rice (sometimes
    called glutinous rice)
1 T. grated organic orange
    peel
1 C. soy sauce, tamari
2 T. honey
2 cloves garlic, minced
2 T. almond oil

Heat soy sauce, honey, orange peel, and garlic in a saucepan over medium heat until the sauce becomes slightly thickened. Cool sauce and spread on duck evenly, inside and out. Refrigerate overnight. Cook the rice with the almonds and apricot kernels until tender.* Stuff the duck and truss. Heat oil in frying pan. Fry duck in pan until light brown, turning duck to brown on all sides. Roast in 300° F. oven for 2½ hours. Chop duck lengthwise, then crosswise in 1-inch slices. Serve on beds of lettuce and alfalfa sprouts. Serve with Chinese Peas.

*To cook the rice put 1 C. rice in casserole and add 2 C. water and 1 t. salt. Cover and bake for 1 hour. Oven temperature should be 350° F. Remove cover and allow to dry out a little. Serves six.

Eggs

Eggs are outstanding in their nutritional benefits, for they are abundant in all of the essential amino acids. The yolk is rich in vitamin E, biotin, choline, inositol, vitamin A, and the sulfur-containing amino acids that are so rare in most foods. The egg white has substantial amounts of riboflavin and the complete protein albumin. Raw eggs give the highest benefits because heat has not altered the vitamin structure. Always eat the white and yolk together. All cooking must be done gently. It is particularly important not to "hard-boil" eggs as the lecithin or cholesterol-protecting substance will be destroyed.

It is the author's opinions that raw or softly cooked eggs from healthy, naturally fed chickens, raised on the ground, are of dietary benefit.

Sweet Omelette

1 drop lecithin liquid
1 t. vanilla extract
1 t. brandy
2 fresh organic fertile eggs
2 T. raw honey
2 T. raw pecans, organic
2 T. raw unsweetened coconut
2 T. organic raisins
    (unsulfured)
Salt to taste, sea salt
½ t. ground *apricot kernels*
1 T. certified raw butter

With paper towels, wipe inside of heavy skillet with drop of lecithin. Separate eggs and beat whites into peaks. Heat pan over medium heat. Have butter ready. Have plate warming. Gently fold beaten yolks into whites. Add vanilla and brandy. Put butter into the pan. It should sizzle but not burn or smoke. Pour in the egg mixture. Cook over medium heat. Tip pan so that the butter and eggs flow over the bottom and half-way up the sides. Lift the edges to let the uncooked egg flow under. Smooth the top of the omelette with your fork and let it rest for a second or two. As soon as the edges appear done and the top is still moist and creamy, sprinkle raisins, nuts, kernels, and coconut on top. Drizzle honey over this. Fold omelette in half. Slide carefully onto plate. Serves one.

Forrest Carter's "Bumpy" Eggs

8 fertile eggs, beaten with a
    fork until frothy
½ C. sprouted *mung beans*
3 ozs. cream cheese, cut into
    small cubes
1½ T. heavy cream
1½ T. sherry wine
2 T. raw butter
4 sprigs *watercress*

Heat butter gently in heavy skillet until it begins to sizzle. Mix eggs, beans, cream cheese, cream, and wine. Pour over butter and cook gently until scrambled. Serve on individual plates with sprig of watercress. Serves four.

Filbert Soufflé

¼ C. ground filberts
2 t. ground *apricot kernels*
3 T. whole-wheat flour (or
   buckwheat flour)
3 T. raw butter
1 C. milk
½ C. dark-brown sugar
4 fertile eggs, separated
½ t. sea salt (add last)

Make a white sauce by
blending flour and butter
together. Then add the milk all
at once, stirring over medium
heat until smooth and thick.
Mix in the sugar, filberts,
apricot kernels, salt, and egg
yolks one at a time. Beat egg
whites until stiff. Fold into
mixture. Pour mixture into a
buttered 2 qt. casserole. Bake
at 375° F. for about 25 to 30
minutes. Top should be golden
and interior tender. Don't
overcook. Serve immediately.
Serves four.

Sprouted Soufflé Non–Dairy & Wheat–Free

1½ C. ground and cooked
   brown rice (see page 112)
½ C. water
½ T. sea salt
4 T. unrefined oil
2 dashes cayenne
1 C. *sprouted mung beans*,
   chopped finely
4 fertile eggs, separated
2 t. ground *apricot kernels*

Warm the rice in a saucepan.
Stir in the water, salt, oil, and
cayenne. Remove from heat
and beat in the egg yolks one
at a time. Fold in the sprouts.
Beat egg whites until very
stiff. Fold rice mixture into
egg whites carefully. Pour into
a well greased soufflé dish and
bake at 300° F. for about 55
minutes. Sprinkle top with
apricot kernels. Serve at once.

Almond Bavarian Cream

2 envelopes (2 T.) gelatin softened in
½ C. cold milk in blender

Add
⅓ C. boiling water and start blender

Add
½ C. honey
4 certified organic fertile eggs
1 T. vanilla
2 t. grated *apricot kernels*
½ C. raw cream (or "imitation cream" and/or almond cream)
Enough milk to make 4 C. liquid

Pour into mold and chill.

Chill four hours or preferably over night. Slightly warm the exterior of the mold with a hot towel and place upside down on a serving plate. Decorate with unroasted almonds. Serves four.

Almond Egg Nog

2 eggs, fresh, fertile
2 oz. raw cream (or home-made "imitation cream")
1 T. *sorghum cane syrup*
1 t. vanilla
½ t. ground *apricot kernels*

Blend at high speed for about 30 seconds in blender. Best if all ingredients are chilled. High in vitamin A and E. High in choline, inositol, biotin, lecithin, riboflavin, B_{17}, iron and other minerals. This makes a quick nourishing breakfast for a nominal cost. About 350 calories. It is very filling and so satisfying. You shouldn't be hungry again 'til lunch time. Serves one.

Almond Custard

4 C. milk (or home-made "imitation cream")*
6 organic fertile eggs, beaten
6 T. *sorghum cane syrup*
2 t. *apricot kernels*, ground

Mix milk, eggs, and syrup well. Place in double boiler and cook over hot water (not boiling) until thick, stirring constantly. Serve over chilled berries. Serves four.

*See page 152.

Sharon's Egg Nog

2 C. raw milk, chilled
2 fertile eggs
1 banana
2 T. *sorghum cane syrup*
2 T. carob powder
1 t. inactive yeast powder, primary or brewers'
2 T. raw wheat germ, fresh
2 T. powdered milk, non-instant
2 t. *apricot kernels*, ground

Blend all the ingredients together in the blender at high speed. Drink at once. Contains about 35 grams of complete protein.

Salads

Salads are superior as a means of serving nutrients necessary for good health. Always try to get a wide variety of fruits or vegetables in each salad serving. The following is a partial list of salad ingredient possibilities:

head lettuce	peas
romaine lettuce	carrots
red top lettuce	tomatoes
bibb lettuce	radishes
endive	bell peppers
escarole	onions
Chinese cabbage	scallions
green cabbage	garlic
red cabbage	celery root
watercress	chives
spinach	chillies
chard	asparagus
dandelion greens	cooked brown rice
water chestnuts	marinated garbanzo beans
shallots	fish
leeks	chicken
celery	roast beef
bamboo sprouts	nuts, whole (e.g. piñon)
alfalfa sprouts	nuts, ground (e.g. *apricot*
lentil sprouts	*kernels*)
mung bean sprouts	marinated "leftovers"
millet sprouts	coconut
buckwheat sprouts	grapefruit
garbanzo sprouts	orange
broccoli	lemon
cauliflower	lime juice

Also: natural sweeteners such as sorghum cane syrup or honey; seeds such as sesame and cardamon; natural herbs such as fennel leaves, sweet basil, oregano, sage, rosemary, and marjoram; natural salt; and unrefined expeller pressed oils such as soy, safflower, corn, and many more.

Be imaginative in your salad making. Develop your own special dressing flavors. A good general rule, however, is not to mix sweet fruit with tart vegetables.

Your vegetables should always be stored in a dry, cold state—not wet! As soon as the vegetable is washed it should be dried before storage. Otherwise, the water withdraws vitamins and minerals from the plant through a process called osmosis, and you lose the benefits you paid for—good nutrition.

"Chickees at the Beach"

1 C. cooked *millet*, using as little water as possible for cooking. Don't over cook.

1 C. *chick peas (garbanzo beans)*, cooked

1 organic lemon, squeezed for juice

Dash cayenne

1 small cucumber, finely diced

1 small onion, finely diced

1 small bell pepper, finely diced

2 large tomatoes, chopped coarsely

4 T. raw sesame oil

1 C. chopped mint

1 garlic clove, minced

1 T. chopped chives (op.)

½ t. cinnamon

Toss all ingredients together and chill. Serve on beds of watercress. Serves four.

Avocado-Fruit Salad

4 avocados, cut into halves

1 lemon, organic

1 C. seedless grapes

2 C. sour cream (or yogurt)

¼ C. grated, unsweetened coconut

4 washed grape or fig leaves

¼ C. fresh blueberries

¼ C. fresh papaya, chopped coarsely

¼ C. shaved, raw almonds

2 t. ground *apricot kernels*

Rub cut sides of avocados with lemon juice. Mix the sour cream lightly with the fruit, two teaspoons lemon juice, and coconut. Place one half avocado on leaf on salad plate. Pile high with mixed fruit. Sprinkle with a mixture of almonds and apricot kernels. Chill thoroughly and serve. Serves four.

Root Salad*

3 white radishes, organic, chopped
3 red radishes, organic, chopped
1 beet, organic, grated
1 small kohlrabi, organic, chopped finely
1 celery root, organic, finely chopped
2 medium carrots, organic, thinly sliced
1 turnip, organic, finely chopped
1 medium onion, finely chopped, organic
4 **beet tops**, finely shredded
1 small head lettuce, chopped
½ C. fresh **spinach leaves**
5 sprigs **watercress**
1 C. **mung sprouts**
1 organic lemon, juice and grated rind
½ C. safflower oil
1 t. sea salt

Chill vegetables. Just before serving, add lemon juice and rind, oil, and salt.

*"Organically grown root vegetables contain orotic acid or B_{13} useful in transporting minerals throughout the body." Dr. Joseph Evers, Arnesberg, Germany.

Almond Cole Slaw

1 medium head cabbage
1 C. unsulfured raisins
1 medium carrot
¼ t. anise seed
2 t. ground **apricot kernels**
1 T. **sorghum cane syrup**
1 T. vinegar
2 T. mayonnaise or more

Finely chop cabbage, raisins, and carrot. (This can be done easily in the blender or food processor.) Mix in the remaining ingredients and chill. Serves six.

Saint Patrick's Day Molded Salad

1½ T. gelatin
½ C. cold water
¾ C. boiling water
2 T. lemon juice, fresh, organic
1¼ t. sea salt
1 t. grated onion
2 dashes tabasco
2½ C. sieved, ripe avocado (about three)
1 C. sour cream (or yogurt)
1 C. home-made mayonnaise
1 C. raw, ground *cashews*
1 C. *alfalfa sprouts*
6 sprigs *watercress*

Soften gelatin in the cold water. Add to boiling water and lemon juice. Stir until dissolved. Cool to room temperature. Stir in the salt, grated onion, tabasco and raw nuts. Blend avocado, cream, and mayonnaise in blender and add. Place in six-cup mold. Chill overnight. Unmold. Place on glass dish in a nest of sprouts with watercress and limes. Serves six.

Festive Apple Salad

4 large red *apples*, unpeeled, cored and chopped coarsely
Seeds of the apple, ground
½ C. fresh organic pineapple chunks
½ banana, chopped
½ C. filberts, chopped, raw
1 T. fresh lemon juice
1 T. grated lemon rind
1 C. home-made mayonnaise
1 bunch *watercress*

Mix all ingredients. Chill. Serve on beds of fresh, crisp, organic watercress.

Chicken Salad I

2 stewing hens, 3 lbs. each
1 head lettuce
1 bay leaf
1 carrot
1 stalk celery
2 C. celery, chopped
1 T. sea salt
1 t. tarragon
1 t. sweet basil
4 C. mayonnaise, home-made
1 jar artichokes
1 small can ripe olives
1 organic lemon
1 C. *macadamias*
1 t. imported olive oil
1 handful organic parsley
2 large organic tomatoes, cut
　　in wedges
Large handful *watercress*
1 C. *alfalfa sprouts*
3 t. *apricot kernels*, ground

Cook chickens with bay leaf, carrot, and celery in pot of water until tender. Drain and cool. Save stock for soup, etc. Cut chicken away from the bones, removing the skin and tendons. Coarsely chop macadamias. Prepare home-made mayonnaise. Chill all the ingredients and prepare to assemble salad. Chop and shred lettuce, leaving some outer leaves whole. Place large lettuce leaves in bottom of large salad bowl. Place chopped and shredded lettuce in next. Layer celery on top. Mix the chicken with the mayonnaise, nuts, salt and tarragon. Place this on top of the celery in the bowl. Place more mayonnaise on top of chicken and decorate with marinated artichokes,* ripe olives, lemon, and tomato wedges. Sprinkle fresh basil over the top. Decorate with the watercress and the alfalfa sprouts. Serves six.

*Marinade: 2 t. wine vinegar, 6 t. olive oil, ½ t. salt, 1 clove garlic, minced.

Carrot Cashew Salad

4 raw organic carrots, grated
½ C. fresh, *cashews*
1 C. unsulfured light raisins
2 T. *sorghum cane syrup*
½ t. cinnamon
½ C. home-made mayonnaise
Pinch sea salt

Mix all ingredients together except raw cashews. Chill. Serve in lettuce cups with nuts sprinkled on top. Serves four.

Cantaloupe Fruit Salad

2 bananas sliced
2½ C. diced fresh pineapple
1¼ C. sliced **strawberries** or **raspberries**
1 T. fresh organic lemon juice
1 C. whipping cream
½ C. toasted coconut
½ C. raw almonds, grated
1½ t. **apricot kernels**, ground
⅛ t. mace
⅛ t. nutmeg
2 cantaloupes
6 grape leaves
6 sprigs of fresh mint

Mix fruits together with lemon juice. Whip cream and mix in the coconut and spices. Just before serving, slice cantaloupes into thirds. Place each on a grape leaf on an individual serving dish. Fill with fruit, dab on the whipped cream. Sprinkle on the nuts and decorate with the mint. Serves six.

Garden Salad

4 C. fresh lettuce
4 small carrots, sliced
1 medium cucumber, sliced
6 radishes, sliced
6 sprigs fresh mint
10 pods fresh green peas
1 stalk raw broccoli, chopped
2 stalks celery, sliced, including leaves
2 large tomatoes, cut into sixths
1 red bell pepper, sliced, include seeds
1 or 2 green chili peppers, small and not too hot
½ C. raw sunflower seeds (contains B_{15}*)
3 t. ground **apricot kernels**
6 sprigs **watercress**
1 C. raw **spinach**

Mix all together in large salad bowl. Chill and serve with vinaigrette sauce. Serves six.

Vinaigrette Sauce:

⅛ C. apple cider vinegar, not distilled
⅜ C. safflower oil
1 t. sea salt
1 clove garlic, minced
1 t. crushed sweet basil

Mix together in small jar and chill beside salad. Don't add until ready to serve. Serves six.

*"B_{15} is useful in transporting oxygen throughout the body." Dr. Ernst T. Krebs, Jr.

French Lentil Salad

2 C. *lentils*, grey-green
Water to cover
¾ t. mace
1 medium onion
1 bay leaf
1 C. fresh mint leaves,
    chopped
½ C. parsley, chopped
4 green onions, chopped,
    including green stalks
1 C. chopped red bell pepper
    including the seeds
¾ C. French dressing
Salt and pepper to taste, sea
    salt

Wash lentils, place in
saucepan with water to cover.
Bring to boil and cook 2
minutes. Turn off heat and
allow beans to soak for 1 hour.
Reheat and add onion, mace,
bay leaf, and cook until just
tender. Drain, saving juices for
soup stock. Gently toss lentils
with mint, parsley, green
onions, bell pepper, French
dressing, salt, and fresh black
pepper. Chill several hours.
Serve on salad greens and
decorate with sprigs of
watercress and alfalfa sprouts.

Bavarian Carrot Salad

½ C. cold water
½ C. boiling water
2½ T. gelatin
½ C. almond oil
6 T. honey, raw
2 t. *apricot kernels*, ground
1 fertile egg
1 can orange juice, frozen,
    unsweetened
1 C. grated carrots

Place cold water in blender,
add the gelatin and turn
blender on to mix. Add the hot
water and remaining
ingredients. Fold in carrots.
Pour into shallow pan and
chill. Cut into squares and
serve on beds of watercress.
Serves four.

Adelle's Greek Salad

1 head lettuce such as bibb, red top, or leaf, washed and drained
1 cucumber, diced
3 ripe tomatoes, segmented
½ lb. feta or cheddar cheese, raw (op.)
½ C. Greek olives
1 medium onion, sliced thinly
½ C. freshly cooked beets, julienne
1 can anchovies
1 jar artichoke hearts
¼ C. capers
1 clove garlic, minced
½ C. olive oil, imported
2 T. wine vinegar
1 t. sea salt
1 t. powdered mustard
1 C. cooked and chilled *garbanzo beans*

Chop lettuce and place in the bottom of a large salad bowl. Place garbanzo beans on top of lettuce. Continue to layer the remainder of ingredients. Make salad dressing by mixing the oil, vinegar, salt, and mustard. Pour over salad and chill for at least one hour. Served by the author at special dinner in her home to a very special guest, Adelle Davis. Serves six.

Wilted Green Salad

2 heads bibb lettuce
1 head romaine, both washed and broken into bite size
10 fresh mushrooms, sliced thinly
10 raw almonds, cracked
Juice of 1 organic lime
1 t. lime rind
1 C. cubed raw cheese
¼ C. brown and bubbly raw butter (or olive oil)
1½ t. *apricot kernels*, ground

Toss all ingredients in a salad bowl except butter. Brown butter and pour over salad at the table. Serve at once. Serves four.

Italian Antipasto Salad

½ C. Italian olive oil
3 T. red wine vinegar
½ t. sea salt
½ C. chilled cooked **garbanzo beans**
2 large tomatoes, sectioned
Freshly ground pepper to taste
1 clove garlic, minced
1 small jar artichoke hearts, drained (save oil) and cut into pieces
1 T. capers
1 small onion, finely chopped
8–12 anchovy fillets
1 mild chili pepper, chopped
½ C. black Italian olives
½ C. sliced green olives
2 T. chopped pimiento
2 T. chopped parsley
1 head romaine
1 bunch **spinach**
6 sprigs **watercress**

Mix oil, vinegar, salt, pepper, and garlic. Heat slightly. Pour over all the vegetables except the tomatoes and marinate for 2 hours. Serve on individual plates on greens. Serves six.

Gelatin Mold for Seafood

½ C. hot tomato juice
1 C. **garbanzo beans**, cooked and chilled
½ C. cold tomato juice
Juice from one organic lemon
¾ C. mayonnaise
1 C. cottage cheese, home-made from yogurt*
½ t. sea salt
1 T. minced **watercress**
1 T. diced green bell pepper
1 T. diced celery

Soften gelatin in blender with cold tomato juice. Add hot tomato juice and liquify. Add mayonnaise, salt, lemon juice, cottage cheese, and liquify again. Pour into a 1½ quart ring mold and chill until "tacky." Fold in the beans, peppers, watercress, and celery. Chill until firm. Serve on bed of lettuce and spinach leaves. Fill center with tuna, crabmeat, or shrimp. Serves six.

*See page 152.

Watercress Salad

1 C. fresh *watercress*, stems removed
1 garlic clove, minced
¾ C. fresh safflower oil
1 large head romaine lettuce
1 C. fresh *spinach*
Fresh black pepper to taste
½ t. sea salt
2 fresh fertile eggs
¾ C. freshly grated cheese
2 C. *millet* dried bread cubes
1 large organic tomato
1 large avocado (op.)

Heat ¼ C. of oil and sauté bread cubes until golden brown. Drain on absorbent paper. Clean and trim greens and break into bite-size pieces. Toss greens with ½ C. additional oil, add salt and pepper. Cook eggs 1½ minutes and break over greens. Add lemon juice and toss gently to mix with eggs. Add croutons, cheese, segmented tomato, and avocado. Serve at once. Serves four.

Salade Niçoise

1 small head soft lettuce such as red top, bibb, leaf, etc.
½ C. *spinach* leaves
10 sprigs each, *watercress* and parsley
2 small cans tuna fish (packed in olive oil best)
3 large organic tomatoes
10 sliced black olives
1 can anchovies
6 T. olive oil
2 T. garlic vinegar
1 clove garlic minced
Freshly ground pepper to taste
½ C. Parmesan cheese
Small jar artichoke hearts

Place washed and drained lettuce in a salad bowl. Add tomatoes cut into sections, tuna, olives, anchovies and artichokes. Refrigerate. Combine oil, vinegar, garlic, and pepper. Refrigerate separately. Pour dressing over salad just before serving and sprinkle with grated cheese. Decorate with sprigs of parsley and watercress. Serves six.

Tabouli Lebanese Salad

2½ C. bulgur wheat with 2½ C. boiling water poured over. Set aside for 1 hour.
4 C. chopped fresh mint, not pressed down
1 bunch chopped parsley (about 3 C.)
10 large scallions, chopped, including stems
4 large chopped onions
½ C. imported olive oil
6 organic lemons, juiced
1 small hot red chili pepper, chopped
Freshly ground black pepper to taste
1½ t. sea salt
½ t. cinnamon
2 t. *apricot kernels*, ground
1 chopped cucumber
4 large tomatoes, cubed

Add all ingredients together. Chill thoroughly and serve. May be made a day early.

Gelatin Mold for Fruit Salads

½ C. cold milk
1 T. gelatin
½ C. hot milk
1 C. whipping cream, raw
8 oz. pkg. cream cheese
½ C. chopped cheddar cheese, raw
½ C. chopped raw almonds
1 t. *apricot kernels*, chopped
½ C. green grapes

Soften the gelatin with cold milk in the blender. Add the hot milk and liquefy. Add the cream and cheeses and liquefy until smooth. Pour into a one-quart ring-mold. Chill until "tacky." Stir in the fruit and nuts. Chill until firm. Turn on to a bed of alfalfa sprouts and mint leaves. Fill the center with fresh berries such as strawberries, boysenberries, blackberries, etc. Serves six.

Carrot Salad

Grated carrots, raisins, raw pecans, mayonnaise, *alfalfa sprouts*, lemon juice, honey, and cinnamon.

Israeli Salad

Chopped cauliflower, celery, cucumbers (all chopped), green peppers, *lentil sprouts*, Swiss cheese cut into strips to form the "Star of David," olive oil, and lemon juice.

Vegetable Bouquet

Sliced raw mushrooms, lettuce, green peppers, cooked and chilled baby *green lima beans*, scallions, egg slices, carrots, and radishes.

Cucumber Salad

Grated cucumber, chopped scallions, *alfalfa sprouts*, and caraway seeds.

Aware Inn Salad

Grated carrot, grated raw beets, cucumbers, celery, avocado, *alfalfa sprouts*, red cabbage, lettuce, tomato, sunflower seeds, and pignolia nuts.

Greek Salad

Alfalfa sprouts, tomatoes, cooked and chilled *fava beans*, cucumbers, Greek olives, feta cheese, mint leaves, and olive oil and lemon juice dressing.

Dinner Salad

Lettuce, carrots, beets, cucumbers, cabbage, celery, *spinach,* and *watercress*. Mayonnaise with 1 t. ground *apricot kernels.*

High-Protein Salad

Egg slices, raw cheese cubes, *alfalfa sprouts*, scallions, raw almonds, cottage cheese, avocado, and tomatoes.

Chinese Salad

Mung bean sprouts, scallions, radishes, celery, bell peppers, raw mushrooms, cauliflower, raw almonds, cucumbers, tomatoes, sesame seed oil, and tamari soy sauce.

Salad Dressings

Salad dressings should be made freshly by you; not bottled or with "packaged" dry herbs. These commercial foods contain preservatives not beneficial to health and even may be adverse. Why spend the money when home-made dressings are so easy to make and so much more delicious and gratifying.

Betty's Green Goddess Dressing

1 C. sour cream (or thick yogurt)
1 stalk celery, cut coarsely
½ bell pepper, cut coarsely
1 large handful *watercress*
1 large handful *spinach*
1 large handful parsley
2 cloves garlic
2 C. home-made mayonnaise

Blend all ingredients together, one at a time, at high speed in blender. Chill overnight. Serve with fruit and vegetable salads. Serves ten.

Sour Cream Salad Dressing I Non-Dairy

2 T. cold water
1 T. gelatin
¾ C. hot water
1 fertile egg
½ C. corn oil
1 t. *sorghum cane syrup*
1 t. "Spike"ing salt*
1 T. apple cider vinegar
1 t. sea salt

Soften gelatin in blender with cold water. Add hot water and blend at high speed until gelatin is dissolved. Add remaining ingredients and chill. If it sets too solidly, add a little water and re-blend. Serves four.

*See page 12.

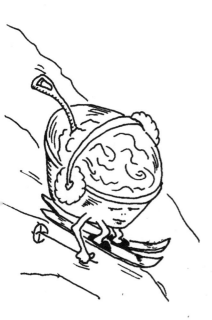

Avocado Almond Dressing or Cold Sauce

2 ripe large avocados, mashed to a pulp
½ C. home-made mayonnaise
1 T. onion, minced
2 t. *apricot kernels*, ground
1 clove garlic, minced
1 t. sea salt
1 T. organic lemon juice, fresh

Blend, chill, and serve. Very good over gelatin salads, cold sliced meat, etc. Serves four.

Sour Cream Salad Dressing II Non-Dairy

1 T. *flax seeds*
¼ C. ground and cooked *millet*
1 egg yolk, (fertile egg)
¼ C. vegetable oil
2 t. apple cider vinegar
1 t. seasoned salt
½ C. water

Grind flax seeds in the blender until finely ground. Add water, then millet and remaining ingredients. Let chill and thicken in refrigerator. Serve over salads or spooned over freshly cooked vegetables.

Basic Vinaigrette

¼ C. vinegar
¾ C. oil
1 t. salt
Pinch of herbs
1 clove of garlic, minced

Variations: tomato paste, onion, spices, horseradish, paprika, mustard, cayenne, honey, capers, chopped egg, Parmesan, pimento, peppers, relish, etc.

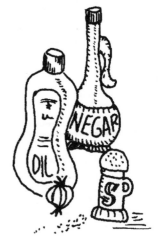

Rémoulade Dressing

⅓ C. tarragon vinegar
2 T. dry mustard
1 t. horseradish
1½ T. tomato paste
1 t. *sorghum cane syrup*
½ t. paprika
½ t. sea salt
¼ t. cayenne pepper
½ C. vegetable oil
¼ C. finely chopped celery
¼ C. finely chopped green
  onions and tops

Combine vinegar, mustard, paste, syrup, paprika, salt, and cayenne. Add the oil, beating constantly until mixed. Stir in the celery and onions. Chill. Serve on shrimp salad, raw vegetables, or other.

Buttermilk Dressing

⅔ C. buttermilk
2 T. horseradish
2 T. tomato juice
1 T. vinegar
1 T. honey
1 t. dry mustard
2 T. Parmesan cheese

Avocado Dressing

¾ C. avocado pulp
Juice of ½ organic lemon
3 T. blue cheese
3 T. heavy cream*
½ t. Worcestershire
½ t. sea salt
1 t. dry mustard

Mash avocado and add lemon. Add crumbled cheese and other ingredients. Chill. Serve on fruit or vegetable salads.

*May substitute oil and/or home-made "imitation cream".

Betty Fay's Shrimp Sauce

1 egg yolk, fertile egg
2 t. anchovy paste
½ t. dry mustard
1 C. home-made mayonnaise
Pepper to taste
1 T. red wine vinegar
1 T. grated onion
1 clove garlic, minced
2 T. dry white wine
    (or apple juice)
1 t. flax seed oil

Beat the egg yolk and add the anchovy paste and remaining ingredients. Blend and refrigerate. Serve as a dip for lightly steamed and chilled shrimp, lobster, and other shell fish.

French Dressing

⅓ C. vinegar
1 clove garlic
4-5 peppercorns
1 C. safflower or olive oil
¼ t. sea salt
⅛ dry mustard
1 t. honey

Combine, mix and chill. Variations: Add Roquefort cheese, paprika, or parsley.

Sherry Dressing

1 fertile egg, beaten
¼ C. **_sorghum cane syrup_**
¼ C. sherry
Pinch of sea salt
2 t. butter
Juice of ½ organic lemon
Juice of ½ organic orange
⅓ C. heavy cream whipped

Combine all ingredients
except the cream in the top of
a double boiler. Stir until
slightly thickened. Chill.
Add whipped cream. Serve
over fruit and other salads.

Caesar Dressing

Blend French dressing in the
blender, add a fertile egg, 5
anchovies, and ⅓ C.
Parmesan. Blend. Chill.

Soups

Soups can be light or heavy, broths or bisques, hot or cold, vegetable, meat or fruit; but no matter how they are made, they can be highly nutritious, or lifeless and deadly.

Long cooking of bones to make stock is a good idea if the animal whose bones you are cooking had a natural diet free from commercial "lures,"* herbicides, pesticides and so forth. Otherwise, some of these substances end up in the animal's skeleton and are released into the broth. You could then be feeding chemicals to your family with cumulative toxic properties.

Another bad practice in making soup is to boil the stock at a high temperature for a long time. This has been known to lock-in the minerals present to such an extent that they cannot be utilized by our systems.

Try to keep all of your foods as organic as possible. Then utilize every scrap. Wash and store all vegetable peelings, tops, etc. in the refrigerator until needed. Boil gently all left-over bones (right from the dinner plates is OK; boiling will kill any bacteria). Save and use as many soaking waters as possible (and all others should be fed to your plants).

Never add fresh vegetables to soups until the end. They should always be a little crisp.

*Lures are esters made in the chemical laboratory. They are imitation foods and flavorings, the purpose of which is to fool us into thinking we are eating something else. They are used also to mask unpalatable foods given to animals. For example, saw dust will be eaten by a chicken when alfalfa lure is added.

Beef Stock (basic recipe)

4 lbs. shin and other marrow bones (cracked)
3 lbs. chuck
2 large onions, quartered
1 turnip
1 bay leaf
10 peppercorns
1 large carrot
6 qts. water
1 C. fresh "greens," *spinach*, *watercress*, celery, leek, parsley, etc.

Garbanzo Bean Soup

1 C. cooked *garbanzo beans*, slightly chopped
4 T. raw butter
2 medium onions. Chop one, slice one thinly
2 t. soy sauce, tamari
2 C. chicken stock
2 slices sour dough, rye, or wheat bread
½ C. Parmesan cheese (op.)

Sauté onions in butter until golden brown. Add soy sauce, chicken stock, and beans and simmer for 20 minutes. Toast bread. Butter it and float it on the soup just before serving. Sprinkle cheese on top and serve at once. Serves two.

Brown bones and beef in oven at 350° F. for about an hour (up to a full day at 200° if time permits). Place in large kettle, add vegetables, and boil gently for about four hours. Remove beef for future use. Strain stock and let cool in refrigerator. Remove fat.

Cream of Chicken and Almond Soup

½ C. ground, unroasted almonds
3 C. chicken stock
1 onion, chopped
¼ C. chopped chicken
1 bay leaf
½ C. milk
2 T. butter
2 T. whole-wheat flour
1 C. cream
2 t. ground *apricot kernels*

Place the stock, almonds, onion, and bay leaf in a saucepan. Heat gently for twenty-five minutes and set aside. Make a cream sauce by blending flour and butter together. Add milk and stir until smooth and hot. Discard bay leaf and strain if desired. Pour cream sauce into stock. Keep heat low and stir constantly for about four minutes. Turn off heat and add cream. Sprinkle top with apricot kernels and serve. Serves four.

Chili Con Carne with Baby Limas

2 lbs. hamburger, freshly ground
2 T. butter, raw, or vegetable oil
2 T. onion, minced
1 garlic clove, minced
½ C. red chili powder, mild (called "California Chili")
2 C. water
1 t. cumin
1 t. oregano
3 T. whole-wheat flour
6 T. water
2 C. baby dried *lima beans*, cooked (also good served instead, over *buckwheat spaghetti*)
Salt to taste, sea salt

Sauté the meat until lightly brown in the butter. Add the onion and garlic. Stir in the chili powder, water, cumin, and oregano. Let mixture come to a boil, reduce heat and simmer, covered, until meat is very tender. Salt to taste. Thicken the sauce before serving as follows: Make a paste with the flour and water. Blend and add all at once. Stir until smooth and thick. Simmer five minutes. Serve with steamed corn tortillas and hot chili salsa.*

*Chili salsa: chop fine and mix: 1 hot chili pepper, 2 raw tomatoes, ½ onion, ½ clove garlic, ½ t. salt, ¼ t. oregano, 1 T. vinegar, ½ bell pepper. Chill for several hours before serving. Serves four.

Lentil Purée

2 C. dried *lentils*
6 C. beef stock or water
1½ T. butter
1 onion, chopped
1 dried hot pepper, crumbled (op.)
½ T. mixed pickling spices
1 bay leaf
¼ t. thyme
Salt and pepper to taste, sea salt

Wash lentils. Cook in stock until tender with spices. Brown onions in skillet with butter. Add to the cooking lentils. Season to taste and press through a sieve. Serve with meat or eggs.

Manila Meatball Soup

¼ C. green beans
4 ears corn including silk
¼ C. *sprouted mung beans*
¼ C. *millet*
1 potato, chopped (don't peel)
1 tomato, chopped (don't peel)
¼ C. unpolished barley
2 carrots, sliced
½ lb. hamburger (or thick
    garbanzo purée)
1 t. butter
½ t. rosemary
½ t. thyme
¼ C. hiziki seaweed (very high
    in iodine)
½ C. miso soy bean paste
    (very high in natural
    enzymes)
2 cloves garlic, minced
6 C. water (or stock)

Cook the corn and silk in simmering water until tender (about four minutes). Remove corn and save. Discard corn silk. Add beans, garlic, millet, potato, tomato, barley, carrots, and seaweed. Start simmering. Make meatballs from the hamburger, mixing in the rosemary and thyme. Brown them in the butter in a small skillet. Add meat and browned butter to the soup and simmer for about 25 minutes. Add miso paste and serve. Serve corn on the side or cut into two-inch pieces and place in cooked soup. Watch soup carefully and add more water if needed. Serves four.

Sandra's Salad Soup

46 ozs. tomato juice
1½ t. sea salt
1 T. dark-brown sugar
1 small garlic clove, diced
    very finely
¼ C. safflower oil
2 T. organic lemon juice
1 t. soy sauce, tamari
1 cucumber, diced
1 green pepper, diced,
    including the seeds
3 tomatoes, diced
1 C. shredded carrots
1 C. celery, diced
1 C. *sprouted mung beans*

Combine all ingredients. Chill in refrigerator for twenty-four hours. Serve in soup bowls.

Lentil Soup with Meat Balls

1 C. dried *lentils*
5 C. water or beef stock
2 T. olive oil or butter
2 onions, coarsely chopped
1 minced garlic clove
2 small bell peppers, chopped
1 small red pepper, dried and
    crumbled (op.)
¼ t. powdered mustard
¾ lb. hamburger
½ C. bulgur wheat or whole-
    wheat bread crumbs
1 fertile egg
Pinch nutmeg, (op.)
½ t. sea salt

In a heavy kettle lightly brown the onions, garlic, celery, and bell peppers. Wash lentils and add. Add water, red pepper, and mustard. Cover and cook gently for about 1½ hours, or until lentils are tender. Make meat balls by mixing egg, salt, and nutmeg with bulgur wheat (softened with an equal amount of boiling water and allowed to stand for thirty minutes) or bread crumbs. Brown in skillet with a little oil. Add to lentils about forty minutes before lentils are done. Serve alone in bowls or with brown rice. Serves four.

Miyeko's Seaweed Soup*

5 C. chicken stock
4 diced raw shrimp
¼ lb. ground chuck
4 C. chopped water chestnuts
    (canned)
1 small can *bamboo shoots*
3 sheets dried Japanese
    seaweed (may be nori,
    kombu, or hiziki) broken
    into small pieces
1 t. sea salt

Wash the seaweed thoroughly in a sieve under running cold water. Soak in cold water for 10 minutes. Drain (save the soaking water for your plants) and add to the stock. Bring to a boil and simmer. Add the remaining ingredients and cook gently for about ten minutes or until they are tender. Serves four.

* High in iodine and zinc.

Fresh Lima Bean Soup

2½ C. freshly cooked *lima beans*
2 C. certified raw milk (or yogurt)
2 T. whole-wheat flour
1 T. *sorghum cane syrup*
2 T. raw butter
1 clove of garlic
1 thin slice onion
¼ t. sea salt
Fresh pepper to taste

Blend the flour and butter in sauce pan. Add the milk and stir until smooth and thick. Set aside. Put the lima beans, salt, pepper, garlic, onion, and sorghum in blender and blend at high speed. Pour hot white sauce in blender. Blend and serve at once. Serves four.

Cold Cumberland Soup

3 C. yogurt
1½ C. sliced organic cucumbers, don't peel
½ C. ground raw almonds or *cashews*
½ t. sea salt
1 t. *apricot kernels*, ground
1 large clove garlic
2 t. chopped chives and/or *watercress*
1 C. cream, raw (or home-made "imitation cream")

Blend yogurt, cucumbers, and garlic in blender. Chill. Just before serving mix in cream and salt. Ladle into bowls. Sprinkle top with nuts, watercress, and chives. Serves four.

Chilled Watercress Soup

2 onions, chopped
2 T. raw butter
2 potatoes, chopped
2 C. raw all-purpose cream
1 C. milk
1 C. chicken stock
¼ t. white pepper
½ t. sea salt
1 C. stemmed and chopped *watercress*
1 T. ground *apricot kernels*

Sauté onions in butter until transparent. Add potatoes, milk, and stock. Cook until the potatoes are tender. Pour contents into the blender. Blend until smooth. Add watercress and blend again. Add cream and chill. Serve in chilled bowls with a sprinkling of freshly ground kernels. Serves four.

"Esau's Pottage" or Mjeddrah

1½ C. red *lentils*
4 C. cold water
1 t. sea salt
2 C. onions
¼ C. olive oil
¾ C. brown rice
½ T. butter, raw
2 C. hot water
1 C. onions
1 T. raw butter
1 C. leaf lettuce
Several *spinach leaves*
1 tomato
1 onion
4 sprigs fresh mint
1 clove minced garlic
6 T. olive oil
4 T. lemon juice, organic
1 t. mustard, powdered
1 t. paprika

This recipe has two parts. The stew and the salad which can be served in separate bowls or the salad served on top of the stew. Soak lentils from 8:00 A.M. until 4:30 P.M. Drain well. Place in large pot and add 4 C. water. Cook gently for about one hour in covered pot. Add salt. Stir occasionally to prevent sticking. Coarsely chop 2 C. onions and sauté in olive oil gently until onions are tender and transparent. Set aside. Place raw rice and butter in skillet and cook for several minutes until rice loses its shine. Add rice, onions, and hot water to cooking lentils. Cook until lentils are soft but not mushy. Water should all be absorbed so be careful. Don't add all of the last two cups of hot water if you don't think it will be needed to absorb the rice. Sauté the final onion in the butter until crisp and brown. Make salad with greens and vegetables. Toss with oil and lemon juice mixture.

To assemble for serving: Place lentil stew in bowls. Sprinkle crisp onions on top. Serve salad on top or on the side. This dish goes well with Greek olives and Syrian bread.

Vegetables

Vegetables should be grown at home whenever possible. By so doing, one can have the assurance that his or her plants will have quality cell structure, high vitamin-mineral content, and freedom from harmful sprays and inorganic fertilizers.

Commercial farm practices today are oriented toward breeding plant species which produce the highest yield for the lowest monetary investment. Although the yield may be high, the vitamin and mineral content may be low, and the plant may not have the high resistance to insect infestation and disease that the original species had.

Commercial farmers have learned that any plant can be forced to grow if three chemicals are supplied, namely nitrogen, phosphorus, and potash or potassium; also that these chemicals could be manufactured inorganically. This was quite an outstanding discovery. Now farmers no longer had to rotate crops to build up the natural nitrogen in the soil and they no longer had to pay for expensive manures for fertilizer. While the resulting crops may be large and colorful, their nutrition content often is inferior to smaller, naturally grown varieties.

There are a number of factors that determine the color, size, texture, flavor, disease and insect resistance, vitamin, mineral, and protein content of vegetables. These are climate, humidity, soil conditions, genetics, light, aeration, and temperature of the soil. Light, for example, is very important for the vitamin C and pro-vitamin A content of plants. The soil, however, is the sole source of all the minerals the plant contains.

Since plants are man's primary source of minerals, it is crucial that these plants be grown in mineral-rich soil. The essential minerals include calcium, phosphorus, sodium, potassium, magnesium, manganese, copper, iron, zinc, iodine, chromium, cobalt, sulfur, molybdenum, and others. There are many instances of mineral deficiencies found in animals as a direct result of mineral deficiencies in the soil. For example, copper-deficient areas exist in the Southeast, notably Florida. Cattle pastured there must be given additional copper if they are to remain healthy.

The absorption of mineral ions by plant roots is a complicated process. All of the facts needed for an adequate explanation are not yet known. Soil structure, pH, soil microorganisms, and moisture exert an influence on this process.

This absorption depletes the soil's mineral supply which must be constantly replenished. To a large extent, commercial farmers are ignoring this need. Even when chemically pure minerals are added to the soil, they seldom supply the soil's total mineral needs. Plants are highly selective; they require minerals in a special assimilable and balanced state. It should be no surprise, therefore, that animal feces and plant refuse supply this optimum state. This is part of the natural cycle of nature. Animals eat plants. Microscopic organisms break down the resulting waste products. Plants then reconstruct this residual soil into food, and the cycle repeats.

With this in mind, let me repeat that, whenever possible, grow your own vegetables and fruits. To do this successfully, one must put manure and decomposing plant substances into the soil. If the soil is completely devoid of nutrients, this building process may take several years. The rewards, however, are well worth the effort.

Manure (sheep, cow, chicken, etc.) and food refuse can be scattered around the base of the plants. Spread all the way out to the "drip-line." Then scatter dried grass and leaves on top. Beneficial insects and microscopic organisms will break the material down and carry it into the soil for the plant's utilization.

Don't remove your vegetables from the garden until you are ready to eat them. This, of course, isn't applicable to winter storage. Wash lightly and don't peel. The skin is rich in nutrients and, many times, coated with wild yeast, abundant in B-complex. Never cook vegetables unnecessarily. Never pre-soak. If necessary, steam quickly and with moderate heat. Don't pressure cook as this exerts too high a heat. Never cook vegetables more than once. Leftovers can be chilled, marinated, and served cold in salads.

Bamboo Shoots

Bamboo shoots are the new growths of the "cane-like" plant that provides a very nourishing food. Bamboo is a giant grass that puts out shoots in the winter and the spring. The shoots are very high in B_{17}. We in the United States get them usually cooked and in cans. The fresh ones can be boiled in salt water until tender. The flavor of the young shoots has been likened to artichokes.

Fresh Asparagus with Almond Butter

2 lbs. fresh asparagus
2 T. raw butter
1 t. *apricot kernel*, ground

Break off tough ends and discard. Steam asparagus in a little water, about ½ C., for three to five minutes. Or steam in steamette. Serve with almond butter. Many vegetables may be substituted for the asparagus, such as broccoli, carrots, beets, spinach, green beans, turnips, chard, etc.

Almond butter: Melt ¼ C. raw butter, gently. Mix in ¼ t. ground apricot kernels. Serve over vegetables. Serves four.

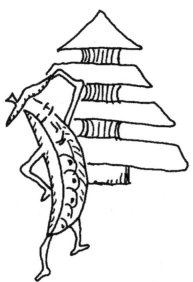

Chinese Peas (Snow Peas)

2 C. Chinese peas (snow peas) "String" and cut large ones in half
1 C. *mung bean sprouts*
1 7 oz. can water chestnuts, sliced
1 C. fresh mushrooms, sliced
1 T. sherry (op.)
1 T. soy sauce, tamari
1 t. honey
1 T. butter
2 T. olive oil, imported
½ C. raw almonds, cracked

Wash and prepare the vegetables. In large saucepan, sauté peas, sprouts, and chestnuts in the olive oil. Do not have the heat too high or they will burn. When vegetables are barely tender add the butter, honey, sherry, and soy sauce. Do not cover. Serve immediately. Serves four.

Stuffed Eggplant

2 small eggplants
4 cloves garlic, minced
1 C. sour cream (or yogurt)
1 C. cubed cheddar cheese, raw
1 C. whole-wheat bread crumbs
2 t. ground *apricot kernels*
2 t. raw butter

Bake halved eggplants until tender, about 25 minutes, in 350° F. oven. Scrape out centers, chop, mix with cheese, sour cream, and garlic. Refill eggplant shells with mixture. Mix apricot kernels with bread crumbs and salt and sprinkle on top. Dot with butter. Bake until hot and brown on top. Serve at once. Serves four.

Skillet Cabbage

1 T. safflower oil
1 C. chopped celery including green leaves
1 green pepper, cut in strips, including seeds
1 small onion, chopped
1 t. sea salt
Freshly ground black pepper to taste
1 C. *sprouted lentils* or *mung beans*
3 C. finely shredded cabbage

Heat in skillet over medium heat in hot oil. Mix in all ingredients well. Cover pan and steam gently five minutes. Serve immediately. Vegetables should be crisp. Do not overcook. Serves four.

Unroasted almonds or grated apricot kernels (2 t.) may be sprinkled on top if desired.

Crêpes

Crêpes are very versatile. They can be served as a side dish, appetizer, main dish, or dessert. They are delicious for breakfast, brunch, lunch, buffet, dinner, or late snack. They are filling and nutritious and are great for leftovers. There are three parts to a crêpe dish: the pancake, which is rich with egg and very thin; the filling, which can be savory or sweet; and the sauce, which is usually rich and heavy with cheese.

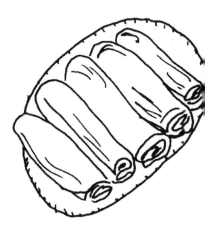

Basic Crêpe

½ C. cream (may include 1 T. sherry or brandy)

6 T. whole-wheat pastry flour

2 fertile eggs

1 T. melted butter

1 T. *sorghum cane syrup* (op.) (for dessert crêpes)

1 t. grated lemon or orange rind, organic (op.)

1 t. vanilla extract (op.) (for dessert crêpes)

Mix in blender. Allow to chill until bubbles disappear. Pour about three tablespoons of mixture in hot small skillet that has been oiled slightly. Coat pan with mixture by tipping and turning skillet. When batter loses shine, bottom should be brown. Flip and brown other side lightly. Flip onto warm platter. May be made ahead of time.

Zanahorias Natas (Braised Carrots)

Clean 12 carrots and cut into julienne strips. Braise slowly in 1 T. raw butter until tender. Add ½ C. *mung sprouts* and cook three more minutes. Top with sour cream and chopped chives. Stir and serve. Serves four.

Florentine Crêpes

3 T. green onion, chopped
1 T. raw butter
2 C. chopped raw *spinach*
2 medium eggs, separated
1¼ C. cottage cheese, home-made
¼ t. nutmeg
Salt and pepper to taste
11 crêpes
2 C. Mornay sauce*

Sauté the onions in butter. Cook spinach and mix with the onions, egg yolk, cottage cheese, and seasonings. Fold in 1¼ C. sauce and egg whites. Fill crêpes, roll, and place in baking dish. Cover with remaining sauce. Bake at 400° F. for about 15 to 20 minutes. Serve with watercress.

*Mornay Sauce: Melt 4 T. butter and 4 T. whole-wheat flour. Add 2 C. light cream and stir until thick. Stir in ⅔ C. Parmesan cheese. Season to taste. Makes two cups. Serves four.

Lima Stuffed Tomatoes

4 large tomatoes
1 C. fresh *lima beans,* organic
½ C. fresh corn, organic, scraped off the cob
1 t. fresh parsley, organic, minced
1 t. ground raw almonds or *apricot kernels*

Hollow out about a two-inch diameter from the tomatoes. Cook the limas. Add the corn and parsley about the last two minutes of cooking. Drain well (saving the vegetable juices for soup). Place in tomato cases. Broil lightly (about three minutes). Sprinkle the nuts on top. Serve. Serves four.

Candied Carrots

Cook 1 lb. fresh carrots in 1 C. water and 2 t. *sorghum cane syrup* until tender. (Save stock.) Place carrots in skillet and add ½ C. vegetable stock, ½ C. dark-brown sugar, and 3 T. butter. Cook slowly for 30 minutes. Sprinkle with ½ C. chopped *raw cashews* and serve. Serves four.

Eggplant Parmesan

½ C. cooked and drained
 garbanzo beans
1 C. olive oil (imported)
2 cloves garlic, minced
1 large onion, chopped
3 large tomatoes, sliced
1 can tomato paste, 15 oz.
1 t. dried basil
1 t. sea salt
Freshly ground pepper to taste
1 medium eggplant, sliced in
 ¼" slices
½ C. grated Parmesan cheese
Small mozzarella cheese,
 sliced
¼ C. raw butter
1 t. dried oregano

Heat ¼ C. of oil in skillet.
Sauté garlic and onion until
soft. Add tomato paste, half of
the herbs, salt, pepper, and
cook gently for about 30
minutes. In a second skillet
heat the remaining oil, a little
at a time, and lightly heat the
eggplant slices for about thirty
seconds on each side. Set
aside. When sauce is ready,
layer slices of eggplant,
tomatoes, mozzarella cheese,
garbanzo beans, tomato sauce
and repeat. Cover top with

sauce and sprinkle with
cheese. Bake at 350° F. for 30
minutes. Variations: chopped
ripe olives, minced clams,
sunflower seeds and/or piñon
nuts. Serves eight.

Baked Tomatoes

5 large organic tomatoes, cut
 into halves crosswise
¾ C. whole-wheat bread
 crumbs
1 T. dark-brown sugar
2 T. unroasted **filberts**
2 t. ground **apricot kernels**
1 t. sea salt
¼ t. sweet basil
¼ t. oregano
1 bunch **watercress**

Place tomatoes in shallow
baking dish. Mix remaining
ingredients, except for the
watercress. Pile lightly on top
of tomatoes. Bake at 325° F.
for about 18 minutes. Serve
decorated with watercress.
Serves five.

Hot Artichokes in Garlic Butter

Trim the sharp points off of the leaves of four artichokes with scissors. Place in steamer upside down. Steam until tender, about 35 minutes. They are done when center leaves pull out easily. Melt ½ C. raw butter in saucepan and add the juice of one lemon, 1 clove of garlic, minced, and 1 T. ground *apricot kernels.* Serve. The tips of the artichoke are dipped into the butter and then scraped off with the teeth. Serves four.

Vegetable Medley*

½ lb. string beans
½ lb. corn
½ lb. tomatoes
½ onion, sliced thinly
1 clove garlic, minced
1 T. raw butter
2 t. ground *apricot kernels*
1 t. sea salt

Combine and gently cook all of the ingredients but the kernels for twenty minutes. Sprinkle in the kernels and serve. Serves four.

*Complementary vegetables that produce a more complete protein dish.

Candied Yams

Cook to a thick syrup 1 C. brown sugar, ½ C. juice such as orange, apple, pineapple, etc., or water. Cook 2 lbs. *yams* by steaming until tender. Peel and brown in 2 T. raw butter. Place in 1½ qt. casserole, sliced in half lengthwise. Add fresh chunks of pineapple. Pour sauce on top. Bake at 350° F. for 25 minutes. Just before serving add ½ C. raw pecans. Serves four.

Sprouts

The art of sprouting is very important to the "natural" cook. Sprouts contain all of the nutrients of the seeds plus vitamins A and C, not present in the unsprouted seed. Also, for those people who love beans and seeds but claim they are too high in carbohydrates, sprouts are just the answer. The sprouts are much lower in carbohydrates. Also, we never know when the occasion may arise when we will be unable to get fresh vegetables. It is comforting to know that, as long as we have a good source of dried nuts, seeds, and legumes, we can always grow our own supply of C and pro-vitamin A. Sprouts are also a marvelous source of B_{17}, minerals, and protein (incomplete). Combine sprouts with grains, such as bread, in sandwiches, etc. to complete the amino-acid group.

Growing sprouts is very simple. First make certain to buy seeds that are fresh and untreated with fungicides. *Alfalfa sprouts* are probably the most gratifying for the beginner; however, *mung*, soy, *lentil*, grain, fenugreek, pea, *garbanzo beans*, etc., all sprout readily.

Place 3 T. *alfalfa* seeds in a quart mason jar with a piece of cheese cloth tied over the top. Soak the seeds overnight and drain in the morning (give the water to your plants). Then rinse and drain thoroughly twice a day for three days. Some people keep the seeds in a dark area. This is not necessary, but do keep them away from direct sunlight. Jar will fill with sprouts. Store in refrigerator. Eat them within a week.

Sprouts will help unleavened bread to rise and will also quicken the rising of leavened bread.

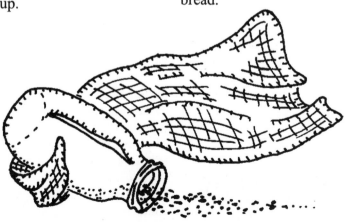

Grains, Seeds and Beans

Cereals and Quick Breads

It's easy to love these foods. Many people, however, avoid them because of their high calorie counts and because they are not complete in the essential eight amino acids. There is no avoiding the first fact, but if you can stand the calories, these foods can be very nutritious simply by using grain and legume combinations that often produce complete protein and by employing whole-grain flours and natural sugars instead of the more refined sugars and starches used today. Such cereals and breads look better, taste better, smell delightful, and, in my opinion, are far better for you.

Baking soda and baking powder, which has baking soda in it, can neutralize the hydrochloric acid in the stomach thus causing indigestion and heartburn and may lead to even more serious gastrointestinal problems. These highly alkaline substances can also destroy a certain amount of the B-Complex in the stomach. For these reasons I recommend that, instead of baking soda, use bakers yeast, stiffly beaten egg white, sparkling wine, beer (the alcohol cooks out), or plain "fizz" water. These methods have been used for centuries and they work very well.

Cereal Suggestions

1. Add 2 t. *apricot kernels*, ground with the *buckwheat groats* then cooked the "instant" way (or add after the cooking). See Ground Cereals-Basic recipe pg. 112.

2. Grind *buckwheat* and *millet* or brown rice together in the blender for a complete protein cereal, then cook the "instant" way.

3. Add rice polish to all "instant" cereals to give B-complex and add *apricot kernels*, ground to all instant cereals to give B_{17}. Add sunflower seeds to provide B_{15}.

4. Add carob and honey to cereals.

5. A teaspoon of liver powder will not be detected in cereals flavored with carob.

6. You will boost the B_{17} content by sprinkling *flax seeds* over the cereal. Flax is also a natural laxative when ground in a blender. After grinding, keep refrigerated to retard rancidity.

7. Left-over cereals can be used as fillers for meat loaves, puddings and cream sauces.

8. Left-over cereal may be mixed with an egg, honey, butter and vanilla to make a delicious pudding.

9. A little instant *flax powder* may be used to thicken cold and uncooked foods.

Almond, Apricot, Cherry, Peach, Plum, and Nectarine Seeds

These seeds are all very closely related and are classified as "drupe" fruits, as they all contain a hard central "pit" which contains the soft seed or kernel inside.

These seeds are most nutritious, containing large amounts of protein (incomplete), vitamin B (including B_{17}), calcium, potassium, magnesium, iron, and phosphorus. A few of these seeds go a long way, however, as they are a highly concentrated food.

As a meat substitute, these seeds are very useful in the vegetarians' diet. Combined with a food from the grass family, such as rice or bamboo shoots, a complete complement of amino acids is formed to produce high-quality protein. Oriental foods often provide this combination.

The bitter almond is high in B_{17}, but the sweet almond has been so highly hybridized that there is very little B_{17} left. Much larger amounts may be eaten, however, and it, too, is beneficial in many ways. For example, a cream made from crushed unblanched almonds is sometimes recommended for the stimulation of milk secretion in nursing mothers and is an easily digested healthful beverage for babies and children.

Buckwheat

Buckwheat is an herb of the genus Fagopyrum. It is a plant that likes a cool climate, and it will grow on the poorest and most arid soils. It grows wild in Central Asia and Siberia where it originated. It is not a member of the family of cereal grasses to which wheat belongs, however. It has triangular seeds and is used as a cereal. Rich in B_{17} as well as other vitamins and minerals, it is a valuable addition to the diet. It will thicken a cream sauce and can be used in place of wheat in almost any dish.

After harvesting, the outer bran is removed and the buckwheat kernels are ground for flour or made into groats. The flour may be light or dark. The groats are prepared by cooking and drying the seeds. By adding hot water or milk, one has an "instant" dish ready to eat or for use with "kasha" dishes.

Buckwheat groats may be brown or white, coarse, medium, or fine.

Flax Seeds

The seeds of the flax plant are called flax seeds. Flax oil must be refrigerated and dated. It may become rancid after six months. These brown shiny seeds have been grown since the Stone Age. They not only provide a very nutritious food but have been important for centuries for their vegetable fiber used to make ropes and linen cloth.

The seeds are high in unsaturated fatty acids, protein (incomplete), phosphorus, niacin, and iron. They contain a moderate amount of B_{17}. They produce a mucilaginous gelatin when soaked in water, cooked, or uncooked which is beneficial to peristalsis of the colon.

The seeds are delicious sprinkled on cereals, cakes and pies, bread and yogurt. Also a tea may be made by mixing 1 T. flax seeds in 2 C. boiling water and boiling for 15 minutes. This tea is so thick it has to be chewed. Also beneficial as a poultice. It soothes sores, boils, and inflammations.

Lentils

Lentils are legumes. They are very nourishing and almost complete protein. Try always to serve lentils with a grain such as rice, wheat, or corn. These two groups complement each other, each having amino acid groups lacking in the other. This results in a more complete protein food. Meat, milk, cheese, and egg, of course, have all of the essential amino acids present already. By adding a little of this group also to your dish, you assure your family a nourishing and completely protein enriched dish.

The lentil seed is small and lens-shaped. It is ripe when it is dried. It is one of the staple foods of Europe and Asia. It is one of the first seed plants recorded by man and is mentioned many times in the Bible.

There are basically two varieties popular in America. One is the orange variety and is referred to as "Egyptian." The other is a little larger, flatter, a grey-green color, and is known as the "French" variety.

Alfalfa

Alfalfa is a leguminous plant that has been cultivated for over two thousand years to forage. Animals have benefitted from its healthful properties and so may you. The roots of the alfalfa plant

grow extraordinarily deep into the earth and are able to utilize the minerals and trace elements unavailable to the more shallow rooted plants. Alfalfa is a rich source of vitamin B_{17}, as well as other vitamins including vitamin K, which is the clotting vitamin, and vitamin U, believed to be helpful in the healing of ulcers. It's also very high in pro-vitamin A, making it particularly beneficial to pregnant and lactating mothers, as it is said to increase the flow of breast milk.

The tender top leaves of fresh alfalfa are delicious served in salads or "wilted" in a warm skillet with a little olive oil.

In addition to fresh alfalfa, other forms are also available, including pill, powder, seed, and tea. The seeds produce tender and sweet sprouts (see sprouting method) which can be used in sandwiches and salads. They also can be used unsprouted to make a delicious tea. One teaspoon seeds to two cups boiling water. The tea, however, usually is made from the dried leaves. It is rather bland and tastes far better when mixed with mint leaves. Steep one teaspoon alfalfa leaves and one teaspoon mint leaves in two cups boiling water for ten minutes.

Miso Soybean Paste

Miso is the vegetarians "yogurt." It is fermented soybeans which have been aged in wooden barrels for three years. It is said to have the same beneficial action on colon bacteria that yogurt has. Most miso is dark and has the same flavor as bouillon. It can be used any time a recipe calls for beef stock or bouillon cubes.

There are several types of miso: Hacho, which is quite heavy and strong in taste; Mugi, which is blended with barley (making a more complete protein) and not as strong in flavor; and Kome, which is made with a blend of brown rice and is the mildest of the three (also is a good amino-acid combination).

Mix one and a half teaspoon miso with a little water and add to 2 cups hot water for an invigorating broth. Be careful never to add the miso until after the heat is turned off, for just as the good bacteria of yogurt would be killed by high heat, so also will the good bacteria of miso be destroyed in the same manner.

Millet

Millet is a small pearl shaped seed belonging to the grass or grain family. It is grown as a cereal in Asia and Africa where it provides a diet staple for one-third of the world's population. It is used mainly in North America and Europe as a forage plant and is highly nutritious.

Millet is not a complete protein food but can be made so by always serving with it seeds from "broad" leaf plants, such as lentils, fava, lima beans, garbanzo beans, buckwheat, etc. Also, its amino acids are more easily utilized if a complete protein is served with it, such as eggs, meat, cheese, fish, etc.

Legumes

Legumes are seeds that split into two halves. They are called dicotyledonous plants, and they include such foods as peas, beans, and peanuts. They are high in carbohydrates, protein (incomplete), certain vitamins, minerals, and a moderate amount of unsaturated fat. Mix them with grains whenever possible to produce a more complete protein. For example: pinto beans with stone-ground corn tortillas, black-eyed peas with brown rice, garbanzo beans with millet, whole-wheat berries with potatoes, and so forth.

Fava Beans

Fava beans are a very rich source of vitamin B (including B_{17}), phosphorus, iron, and calcium. They are sometimes called broad beans and have been cultivated in Europe since the Iron Age. They are particularly popular in Italian and Lebanese cooking. They are quite high in B_{17}. Therefore, one serving a day would be quite sufficient. Cook them with soups and spicy sauces, as they are rather bland.

Garbanzo Beans

Garbanzo beans grow several to the pod and are a valuable food, rich in calcium, potassium, sodium, iron, phosphorus, B_{17}, and protein (almost complete). When mixed with seeds, such as sesame seeds, or with grains, such as millet, they more closely compare with the complete protein of meat and meat by-products.

They are available to us only in dry form and must be soaked in water overnight and then simmered for 3 hours (or until tender) before serving.

Garbanzos are sometimes referred to as chick-peas. When mixed with rice, chicken broth, a few herbs, they make a delicious soup. They also are good in antipastos and soups.

Try the Mid-Eastern dish called "Hummus." It makes a very tasty dip.

Super Cereal

4 T. *mung bean sprouts*
1 T. sunflower seeds
1 T. ground raw unblanched almonds
1 t. *apricot kernels*, ground
1½ T. washed unsulfured organically-grown raisins.
½ C. whole raw milk (or almond cream)
1 T. carob powder (op.)
1 T. raw gland or liver powder (op.)

Place foods in a bowl and pour milk over all. Eat slowly, chew thoroughly.

Breakfast Puffs

1 C. cream of rice, home-made (or other whole grain, cooked cereal)
1 T. melted butter
½ t. sea salt
1 fertile egg, separated
1 t. vanilla
1 T. *flax seeds*

Mix all the ingredients except the egg white. Beat the egg white until it stands in peaks. Fold into mixture. Bake on hot griddle until golden brown. Griddle should be at 375° F. Serve with sorghum cane syrup.

To the Milky Way

CC

Yin Yang Wellness
12131 Westheimer, Unit F
Houston, TX 77077
281-558-8989

Celestial Cereal

¼ C. sunflower seeds
¼ C. unroasted almonds
1 t. ground *apricot kernels*
1 T. chia seeds
¼ C. unpolished sesame seeds
1 T. *flax seeds*
½ banana, sliced
3 dates, chopped
1 apple, *including seeds,*
    finely chopped
½ C. milk, raw or "imitation
    milk" (see milk recipes)

Grind the first six ingredients
in blender at high speed. Pour
into cereal bowl. Add fruit.
Pour milk over and eat slowly,
chewing thoroughly.

Flax Seed Pudding

1 fertile egg
½ C. honey
1 t. ground *apricot kernels*
1 C. *flax seeds*
¼ C. sesame seed oil
1 t. vanilla
2 C. raw milk (or home-made
    "imitation cream")

Mix first six ingredients in
blender at high speed. Slowly
add milk. Pudding will thicken
as flax is ground. Serve at
once or chill.

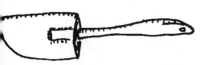

GRAINS, SEEDS, AND BEANS / 103

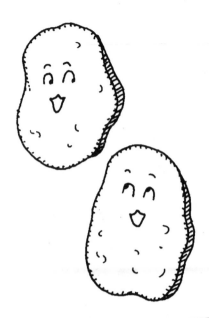

Sourdough Buckwheat Pancakes

1¼ C. **buckwheat flour**
2 T. active dry yeast
2½ T. unsulfured **sorghum molasses**
⅔ C. very warm water
1 large fertile egg, beaten
½ C. sour dough starter*
⅔ C. buttermilk, raw
2½ T. safflower oil
¾ t. sea salt

Stir dry yeast into buckwheat flour. Add very warm water, then remaining ingredients. Place in warming oven for 45 minutes to an hour at a temperature of not more than 120° F. Stir down and bake on a hot griddle at 375° F.

*The sour dough starter is not essential to this recipe since the buttermilk will give a sour dough taste. Substitute by using ½ C. more buttermilk in place of the ½ C. sour dough starter. Serves four.

Cranberry Panpuffs — Dairy-Free

½ C. "ground" and cooked **buckwheat groats,** salted (see instant cereals)
2 fertile eggs, separated
1 t. **apricot kernels**
¼ C. unrefined soy or corn oil
1 T. honey or **sorghum cane syrup**
1 T. vanilla extract
½ C. **cranberries**

Beat egg whites until very stiff. Beat egg yolks and remaining ingredients into cooked cereal. Fold into whites. Bake on hot grid at 375° F. Serve with plum jam and yogurt.

Nancy's Meatless Meatballs

2¼ C. whole-wheat cracker crumbs

1½ C. ground raw nuts (almonds, *cashews*, walnuts, etc.)

2 t. seasoned salt (such as home-made "Spike"ing Salt), see pg. 12

1 large onion, minced

3 t. sage

1½ C. grated raw cheddar cheese

3 garlic cloves, minced

6 T. minced parsley

8 fertile eggs

2 t. *apricot kernels,* ground

Combine all ingredients and blend in eggs. Form into walnut sized balls and freeze overnight.

2 t. miso soy bean paste

2 C. boiling water (may be partly wine or apple juice)

2 T. whole-wheat flour (or *buckwheat flour*)

4 T. raw butter

Lightly brown flour in hot dry skillet. Add butter and make a paste. Mix in liquid all at once and bring to boil. Stir until thick and smooth. Blend in the miso. Place meatballs in a casserole and pour gravy over them. Bake in the oven for 1 hour at 350° F.

Brown Rice Casserole

1 C. long grain brown rice

2½ C. beef broth or water

½ C. slivered, unblanched, unroasted almonds

2 t. *apricot kernels,* ground

2 T. chopped onion

2 T. chopped bell pepper

3 T. raw butter

3 T. chopped parsley

Brown vegetables, almonds, and rice in the butter. Place in casserole with water, cover and bake at 350° F. for 1¼ hours. Sprinkle with ground apricot kernels and parsley.

Curried Lentils from India

1 C. orange *lentils*
1 C. milk, raw (or yogurt)
½ C. grated raw coconut
½ C. unsulfured white raisins
1 onion, chopped
2 T. sesame oil
2 C. beef stock or water
1 T. curry powder
1 T. *sorghum cane syrup,* or honey, raw
2 T. fresh organic lemon juice
1 t. grated organic lemon rind
Salt and pepper to taste, sea salt
2 C. steamed brown or "sweet" rice

Soak washed lentils, milk, coconut, and raisins in refrigerator overnight. Brown onion in oil. Place lentil mixture in heavy saucepan. Add onions, beef stock, curry, and syrup. Cook gently until lentils are tender. This takes about 1½ hours. Season to taste. Gently stir in the lemon juice and rind. Serve in bowls over rice. Unroasted almonds, fresh unsweetened coconut, chopped scallions, and unsulfured currents may be served on the side.

Buckwheat Pizza Crust

1 T. active dry yeast
¼ C. warm water
1½ C. hard whole-wheat flour
½ C. *buckwheat flour*
1 t. sea salt
1 T. almond oil

Dissolve yeast in ¼ C. warm water. Add remaining ingredients. Knead on floured board until smooth and elastic, adding more whole-wheat flour if needed. Let rise in warming oven one hour. Knead down. Divide into two balls. Roll out to fit pizza pie pans. Let rise again 30 to 45 minutes. Fill and bake. May be frozen (see recipe for Garbanzo Pizza). Two pies.

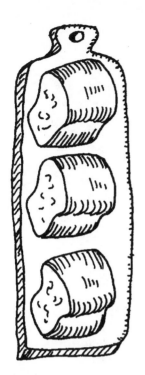

Sour Dough Millet Bread

In a small bowl mix:

2 T. granulated active yeast
6 T. *sorghum cane syrup*
½ C. warm water

In a saucepan bring to steam heat:

1 qt. buttermilk
2 T. sea salt
6 T. oil

When milk mixture is cool and yeast mixture is bubbly, mix together. Gradually add:

1 C. *millet*
½ C. sunflower seeds
8 C. (approximate) hard, stone-ground 100% whole-wheat flour. (Use only enough to make a firm, manageable dough.)

Place dough on a floured board. Knead 10 minutes. Put dough in large, well greased bowl. Oil top of dough. Cover with damp cloth and let rise in warm place for 45 minutes. Punch down. Knead 1 minute, divide and place into three medium sized well greased loaf pans. Let rise again for 45 minutes. Bake for thirty minutes in a 375° F. oven. Turn out immediately and cool on wire racks.

Millet Griddle Cakes

2 T. active dry yeast
¾ C. very warm water
3 fertile eggs, beaten
1 C. stone ground whole-wheat flour
1 C. cooked *millet cereal*
2 T. honey
¼ C. melted raw butter
1½ C. raw milk

Dissolve yeast in warm water. Add remaining ingredients. Place in warm area for one hour. Stir down. Bake on hot griddle, 375° F. or until drop of water bounces on top of griddle in a little ball. Serves four.

Sour Dough Starter

1 T. active dry yeast
2½ C. very warm water from boiling potatoes
2 C. whole-wheat flour (not pastry or buckwheat flour)
1½ T. **sorghum cane syrup**

Stir yeast into flour. Add water and syrup. Beat until smooth. Place in very large crock or bowl as it will grow quite a bit at first. Cover with light towel and let stand at room temperature for 5 to 10 days, stirring 2 to 3 times a day. Cover and refrigerate until ready to use.

To keep starter going: Add ¾ C. water, ¾ C. whole-wheat flour, and 1 t. syrup to remaining starter after some is used. Let stand at room temperature until bubbly and well fermented, which will be at least one day. Cover and refrigerate until used again. Add a little syrup every ten days even if not used. About four cups.

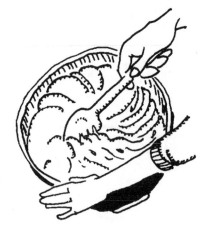

"Peasants" Pancakes

1 C. **buckwheat flour**
¼ C. cream of rice,* home-made (or other whole grain cooked cereal)
1 C. buttermilk, thin yogurt, or water (buttermilk will give a sour dough taste)
2 T. butter or oil
2 fertile eggs, separated
1 t. sea salt
1 T. **flax seeds***

Mix all the ingredients together, except the egg whites. Beat the egg whites until they stand in peaks. Fold into the flour mixture. Bake on a hot griddle until golden brown. The griddle should be 375° F. Serve with butter (op.) and sorghum cane syrup. Serves four.

*Helps to complete the protein of buckwheat.

Polish Blini

1 C. certified raw milk,
   warmed to about 110° F.
   (or water)
1 T. active dry yeast
1½ C. *buckwheat flour*
½ t. sea salt
1 T. *sorghum cane syrup*
3½ T. raw butter (or oil)
3 fertile eggs, separated

Mix flour, salt, and yeast
together. Stir in the hot milk,
syrup, egg yolks, and butter.
Place in warm area (about
110° F.) for about 1 hour.
Beat egg whites until stiff.
Fold into batter. Drop by
tablespoonful onto a hot
greased griddle (about 375°
F.) Turn when brown. Serve
with melted butter and sour
cream, sorghum cane syrup,
or with caviar, smoked
salmon, chopped onion,
firmly cooked egg (chopped
and sieved), capers, sturgeon,
etc. Serves four.

Buckwheat Granola

Combine in a large bowl:
¼ C. *buckwheat flour*
¼ C. *flax seeds*
¾ C. cut unblanched almonds
   (unroasted)
3 T. ground *apricot kernels*
1 C. non-instant powdered
   milk (op.)
4 C. rolled oats
¾ C. unhulled sesame seeds
1¼ C. grated unsweetened
   coconut
1 C. soya powder, (Fearn's)
1 C. wheat germ

In a separate container
combine:

1¼ C. *sorghum cane syrup*
1 C. unrefined safflower oil

Combine dry with moist
ingredients, spread on two
cookie sheets and bake at
300° F. for 15 or 25 minutes,
or until slightly brown. Place
into container for storage.
Store in cool dark place.
May eat dry or serve in bowl
with milk. Twelve cups.

Quick Buckwheat Bread

3 T. active dry yeast
5 C. whole-wheat flour
1½ C. **buckwheat flour**
2 T. sea salt
⅓ C. **sorghum cane syrup**
4 T. unrefined oil
3 C. very warm water

Mix the yeast, the flours, and the salt together. Mix in the water, syrup, and oil and stir. Let rest for about ½ hour and then knead for about 10 minutes. Place in oiled bowl. Oil the dough and place in warm area for about one hour, covering the bowl with a damp towel. Dough should be about double in size after an hour. Punch down and knead (without more flour) for about three minutes and shape into five balls. Place one ball in each of five 1 pound coffee cans, which have been oiled and then dusted with corn meal. Place cans in a warm area covered with a damp towel and allow to rise until the dough lifts the towel. Bake in preheated 425° F. oven for 15 minutes. Then, turning the oven down to 350° F., bake for about 30 minutes. When done, remove from oven. Butter top crust. Turn bread out on rack to cool. May be frozen. Makes five small loaves.

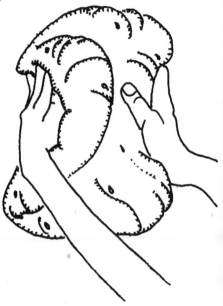

Almond Noodles

½ lb. whole-wheat (or **buckwheat**) noodles
¼ C. chopped parsley
¼ C. chopped unroasted almonds
2 T. dried mint
4 sprigs fresh **watercress**
1½ t. ground **apricot kernels**
1 t. sea salt
1 T. raw butter

Cook noodles in a large pot of boiling water until tender. Drain well and place back into pot. Toss with butter to coat. Add remaining ingredients and toss well. Place in serving bowl and decorate with watercress. Serves three.

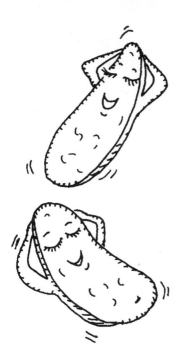

Feathery-Light Buckwheat Pancakes

2 C. *buckwheat* cream sauce, home-made (see sauces)
¾ C. *buckwheat flour*
2 fertile eggs, separated
½ t. sea salt
1 T. *flax seeds* (if not in the cream sauce)

Add the flour, egg yolks, salt, and flax to the cream sauce. Beat the egg whites until they stand in peaks. Fold into the flour mixture. Bake on hot griddle at 375° F. Serve with plum purée and sour cream. (op.) Serves four.

Home-Made Buckwheat Noodles

2 fertile eggs
⅓ C. non-instant, non-fat milk powder
1 t. sea salt
½ C. whole-wheat pastry flour
1 T. ground sage
1 C. *buckwheat flour*
2 t. ground *apricot kernels* (op.)

Beat the eggs, stir in the powdered milk, salt, apricot kernels, and enough buckwheat flour to make a stiff dough (may not need whole cup). Knead and roll 1/16″ thick on pastry cloth with a cloth covered rolling pin. Cover cloth with some of the whole-wheat flour before rolling. You may not need to use all of the wheat flour. Let the noodles "set" for five minutes, then cut into strips ¼″ wide. Dry ½ hour. Put noodles into a rolling, boiling pot of water or broth. Drop noodles in so slowly that boiling does not stop. Reduce heat, and add the sage. Cover the pot and simmer for about 11 minutes. Drain off water (save for plants). Lightly toss the noodles with a little oil or raw butter. Serve with beef and lamb dishes.

Ground and Cooked Cereals, Basic Recipe

The following grains and seeds can be ground in the blender and then cooked "instantly."

Barley
Wheat
Millet
Flax
Buckwheat
Rice
Corn
Rye
Oats
Soybeans (grind and toast in dry skillet before cooking)
Sunflower seeds
Sesame seeds
Chia seeds
Pumpkin seeds

Place 2 cups cold water and 1 t. sea salt in saucepan. Pour in the "ground" grain. Turn on to a medium heat and stir constantly until the gruel comes to a boil. Stir until thick and smooth. This takes only about five minutes.

Potent Protein Powder

2 C. inactive dry yeast powder
2 C. toasted wheat germ
½ C. non-instant, non-fat milk powder (op.)
4 T. calcium gluconate
2 t. magnesium oxide powder
2 C. dark-brown sugar, if sweetness is important
2 C. whey powder (op.)
2 C. powdered whole egg (op.)
½ C. soya powder (soya powder is roasted and does not have that "raw bean" taste)

Mix all together and store in large container in cool dry place. 1½ C. mix added to 1 quart raw milk or water.*

*For dairy-free diets.

Colorado Baked Limas

2 lbs. small dried *lima beans*
Water to soak
Fresh water to cover
2 T. raw butter (or oil)
1 onion
½ t. sea salt
½ C. *sorghum molasses*
Freshly ground black pepper
    to taste
1 can tomato paste
1 T. honey
½ t. all spice
¼ t. clove
1 T. soy sauce, tamari
1 T. Worcestershire
1 T. dry mustard

Wash beans. Cover with cold water and soak overnight. In the morning, drain, cover with fresh water, and cook slowly until tender. Drain, but reserve water. Place beans, butter, and whole onion in bean pot. Make sauce with molasses, paste, honey, all spice, clove, etc. Pour over beans. Add enough cooking water to cover beans. Bake with lid on for five hours, off for one hour at 300° F. Serve with steamed brown bread and garden salad.

Succotash I*

4 C. fresh green *lima beans*
2 ears fresh corn
Water to cook
½ t. sea salt
1 T. fresh raw butter (or oil)
½ C. sour cream (or yogurt)
¼ t. dill weed

Cook lima beans in about 1″ of water until tender. Scrape or cut kernels of corn from cob. Add to the beans along with salt, butter, and sour cream. Place in serving dish and sprinkle with dill weed. Serve with fish and an egg salad. Serves six.

*Beans and corn complement each other's amino acid deficiencies.

Barley Nut Pilaf

½ C. chopped nuts, raw
    (almonds, *cashews*,
    walnuts, pecans)
1 C. barley, unpearled
4 chopped fresh mushrooms
¼ C. dried, crushed mint leaf
1 T. chopped parsley
2 C. beef stock
2 T. raw butter
1 T. beef extract or miso
    soybean paste
1 T. *flax seeds* (op.)
1 T. *apricot kernels,* ground

Melt butter in saucepan. Add onion, mushrooms and sauté gently until lightly browned. Place in casserole with remaining ingredients and cover tightly. Bake at 350° F. for 45 minutes to 1 hour or until barley is tender and liquid is absorbed, sprinkle in flax seeds and kernels. Serve with veal or lamb. Serves four.

Raw Cereal

1 T. *flax seeds*
½ t. ground *apricot kernels*
3 t. rice polish
1 t. inactive yeast (Brewer's or
    primary)
5 T. *lentil sprouts* or *alfalfa*
    sprouts
3 T. ground raw almonds
3 T. unsulfured raisins
Honey to taste (op.)

Mix in bowl with milk or yogurt. Serves one.

Spaghetti Sauce with Lentils

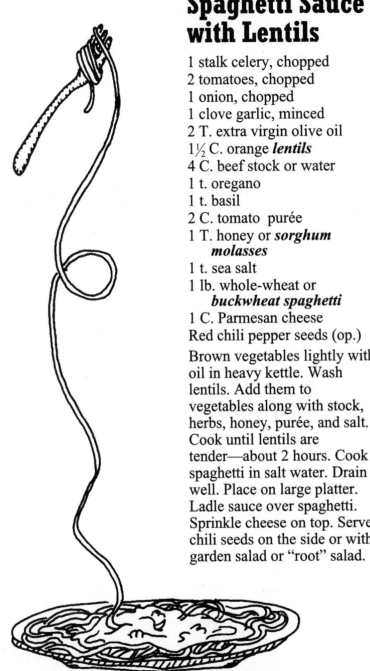

1 stalk celery, chopped
2 tomatoes, chopped
1 onion, chopped
1 clove garlic, minced
2 T. extra virgin olive oil
1½ C. orange *lentils*
4 C. beef stock or water
1 t. oregano
1 t. basil
2 C. tomato purée
1 T. honey or *sorghum molasses*
1 t. sea salt
1 lb. whole-wheat or *buckwheat spaghetti*
1 C. Parmesan cheese
Red chili pepper seeds (op.)

Brown vegetables lightly with oil in heavy kettle. Wash lentils. Add them to vegetables along with stock, herbs, honey, purée, and salt. Cook until lentils are tender—about 2 hours. Cook spaghetti in salt water. Drain well. Place on large platter. Ladle sauce over spaghetti. Sprinkle cheese on top. Serve chili seeds on the side or with garden salad or "root" salad.

Millet Cereal I

¾ C. *millet*
2 C. cold water
1 t. sea salt
1 T. *flax seeds* (op.)

Slow method: Soak millet in water overnight. In the morning cook in soaking water until tender.

Quick method: Grind dry millet in blender at high speed for 1 minute. Mix with flax (op.), cold water, and salt. Heat to boiling, stirring constantly. Simmer 2 or 3 minutes, stirring to keep smooth. Serve with milk and honey. Serves three. (Soaked or ground)

Millet Cereal II (whole grain)

1 C. *millet*
2 C. cold water
1 t. sea salt

Mix ingredients and bring to a gentle simmer. Cook for about 20 minutes in covered saucepan, stirring occasionally. Serve in bowl with milk and sorghum cane syrup. Dried or fresh fruit may be added.

May be served for supper as a side dish instead of potatoes. May be served in stews, pilaf, puddings, and as a filler in meat loafs, etc.

Millet Stew

1 C. *millet*
1 onion, chopped
1 stalk celery, chopped
1 carrot, chopped
1 t. sea salt
5 T. corn oil
5 C. stock or water
1 T. miso or tamari soy sauce

Brown millet in a dry skillet. Remove and add the oil and onion. Brown lightly, adding the celery and carrot near the end. Add stock and millet and cook, covered for about 40 minutes. Serve with green salad and custard pie. Serves four.

Millet Pillau

1¼ C. *millet*
1 onion, chopped
1 T. barley "miso" soybean paste or soy sauce, tamari
2 T. raw butter
3½ C. chicken stock, beef stock or water
½ C. grated carrot

Brown millet for several minutes in dry hot skillet. Add other ingredients and simmer gently for 15 minutes. Serve with meat and garbanzo salad.

Mung Bean Sprouts

4 C. *mung bean sprouts*
1 small can of *bamboo shoots*
2 T. toasted sesame seeds
3 scallions, chopped
1 small can water chestnuts, chopped
1 stalk celery, chopped
1 t. sea salt
Dash cayenne pepper
1 T. sesame oil
3 T. soy sauce, tamari
1 T. arrowroot
3 T. water

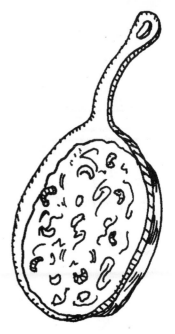

Place the drained vegetables in a heavy skillet with the oil and water. Cover and turn on heat to medium high. Steam for four minutes. Remove vegetables to warm platter. Mix the soy sauce and the arrowroot. Add to the juices in the skillet. Stir over medium heat until thick and clear. Pour over the vegetables. Sprinkle with the sesame seeds and serve. Serves four.

Fresh Lima Bean Salad

2 C. *lima beans,* cooked
½ C. celery, chopped
1 onion, minced
½ cucumber, diced
4 radishes, diced
½ C. red bell pepper, chopped (or green pepper)
2 tomatoes
4 sprigs *watercress*
½ C. mayonnaise (or to taste)

Mix the lima beans with the celery, onion, cucumber, radishes, bell pepper and mayonnaise. Chill. Decorate serving platter with tomato wedges and watercress. Serves four.

Baked Beans, Southern Style

1 pound *shell beans* (or *black* or *fava*). Soak over night. The next day, gently cook 2–3 hours or until tender. Save 2 C. of stock. Place in cooking water: 1 bay leaf, 1 carrot, 1 chopped onion, one garlic clove, and 1 stalk of celery.

2 cloves garlic, minced
1 onion, sliced
1 small dried hot red pepper
1 bay leaf
3 T. *sorghum cane syrup*
¼ C. tomato paste
1 t. powdered mustard
½ t. ground ginger
1½ t. Worcestershire sauce
½ t. sea salt
3 T. Barbados molasses
2 C. stock from the beans

Place drained beans in bean pot. Add 2 C. liquid saved from the cooking beans. Mix other ingredients and pour over the beans. Cook 6 hours covered at 300° F. and one hour uncovered. Serves eight.

Garbanzo Bean Soup

1 C. cooked *garbanzo beans,* slightly chopped
4 T. raw butter
2 medium onions. Chop one, slice one thinly
2 t. soy sauce, tamari
2 C. chicken stock
2 slices sour dough, rye, or wheat bread
½ C. Parmesan cheese (op.)

Sauté onions in butter until golden brown. Add soy sauce, chicken stock, and beans and simmer for 20 minutes. Toast bread. Butter it and float it on the soup just before serving. Sprinkle cheese on top and serve at once. Serves two.

Pizza Crêpes

1 C. *garbanzo beans,* mashed
1 C. chopped onions
2 T. imported olive oil
1 T. anchovies (op.)
2 C. tomato paste, thick
2 C. tomato sauce*, thin
2 C. mozzarella cheese, cubed
1 C. Parmesan cheese, grated
2 small dried red chili
    peppers (op.)
2 t. crushed oregano
2 t. crushed basil
16 crêpes

Sauté onions in the oil. Add the beans, anchovies, thick tomato paste, mozzarella cheese, chili pepper, oregano, and basil. Place 2 tablespoonfuls of mixture in center of each crêpe and roll. Place in buttered baking dish. Cover with the thin tomato sauce and Parmesan cheese. Bake at 450° F. for about 15 minutes.

*Tomato Sauce: Sauté 2 cloves minced garlic and 1 chopped onion in 3 T. imported olive oil. Add contents of 15 oz. can tomato purée, 1 t. crushed basil, 1 t. crushed oregano, and 1 t. salt and pepper. Cook covered for thirty minutes, stirring occasionally.

Marinated Garbanzo Beans

4 C. cooked *garbanzo beans,*
    well drained
¼ C. red wine vinegar
2 T. Burgundy wine
2 T. imported olive oil
½ C. unrefined vegetable oil
1 T. oregano
1 T. basil
2 cloves garlic, chopped
1 T. tarragon
1 t. sea salt

Place the beans in a quart jar. Mix the remaining ingredients together and pour over the beans. Refrigerate for several days. Serve as a garnish or mixed in a salad. Serves four.

Garbanzo Bean Soufflé

3 C. *garbanzo bean* pulp*
3 fertile eggs, separated
1 T. onion, grated
2 T. parsley, chopped
1 T. soy sauce, tamari
½ t. sea salt
1 t. basil
1 t. oregano

Beat the egg yolks and combine with the remainder of the ingredients, except the egg whites. Beat the egg whites until they stand in peaks. Fold into the bean mixture. Pour into soufflé dish or casserole and bake in oven at 325° F. for about 40 minutes. Eat at once.

*Lima, shell, or fava beans may be substituted. To make a pulp: Cook beans and then mix thoroughly in the blender at high speed.

Fava Beans and Brown Rice*

2 C. *fava beans* or other beans
2 T. butter, raw
1 onion, chopped
2 C. brown rice
1 T. sea salt
Freshly ground black pepper to taste
1 hot red pepper

Bring beans and 3 quarts water to boil. Cool for 2 minutes. Cover pan and let stand for 1 hour. Brown onion in skillet and cook until tender. Put on top of beans and cook beans again until almost tender. Add rice and chili pepper and cook until rice is done. Add salt and serve. Serves ten.

Addition: Freshly chopped tomato may be stirred into pottage just before serving if desired. Also 1 t. oregano and 1 t. basil.**

*Beans and rice complement each other in amino acids to make a more complete protein.

**Fava beans are a little more bitter than their cousin the lima. Herbs help to mask this bitterness.

Bean and Barley Stew

2 C. *lima beans*,* soaked
    overnight
½ C. unpearled barley
½ C. carrots, grated
¼ C. onions, chopped
¼ C. *sprouted mung beans*
¼ C. celery, diced
2 T. soy sauce, tamari
2 T. miso bean paste (op.)
2 t. sea salt
1 bay leaf
1 C. grated cheddar cheese,
    raw

Cook all the ingredients
together, except the cheese,
for about 2½ hours. Serve in
individual bowls with cheese
sprinkled over the top. Serves
four.

* Fava, shell, or garbanzo
beans may be substituted.

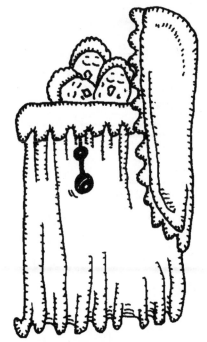

Snap-Beans and New Potatoes

1 lb. string beans
4 small Red Bliss potatoes
2 t. ground *apricot kernels*
Sea salt to taste

Place beans and potatoes in
pot with enough water to
steam gently until tender. This
will take about 40 minutes.
Serve at once with fresh raw
butter and ground apricot
kernels sprinkled on top.
Serve with freshly baked
stone-ground corn bread.*
Serves four.

*Beans, potatoes, and corn
complement each other to
form complete protein.

Garbanzo Pizza

2 6 oz. cans tomato paste
2 cut up tomatoes
1 T. oregano
1 T. sweet basil
Sea salt to taste
½ C. ***garbanzo purée,*** thick*
Pepper, freshly ground, to
    taste
2 cloves garlic, minced
½ lb. Parmesan cheese, grated
2 medium (6 oz. each)
    mozzarella cheese balls
½ lb. fresh mushrooms
1 can anchovies (op.)
4 oz. olive oil, imported

Make one recipe of buckwheat pizza. Drizzle oil onto dough. Mix tomato paste with garlic and garbanzo purée. Spread over the oil. Arrange the remaining ingredients over the paste, sprinkling the cheese and herbs over all. Bake at 425° F. for about 30 minutes. Two pies.

*Make purée by soaking beans several hours or overnight and then cooking until tender. Drain and purée in the blender using a little of the cooking water.

Lebanese Hummus

2 C. ***garbanzo beans,*** cooked
    (marinated ones even
    better)
½ C. sesame or olive oil,
    imported
⅓ C. fresh organic lemon juice
3 cloves garlic
1 t. sea salt
½ C. sesame seeds, unhulled

Place all the ingredients in blender and blend at high speed. Chill. Serve on bread, crackers, or as a dip. About two cups.

Succotash II*

2 C. fresh green *lima beans*
Water to cover
1 t. sea salt
4 ears of corn
⅓ C. raw cream (or
    home-made "imitation
    cream")
2½ T. butter, raw
2 t. ground *apricot kernels*

Place beans in saucepan with enough water to cover. Add salt and cook until beans are tender—about 25-30 minutes. Cut corn from cobs and scrape cobs with soup spoon to get the rest of the corn out of the cobs. Add this to the beans. Cook three more minutes. Add cream, salt and pepper and serve at once, sprinkled with apricot kernels over the top. Serves four.

*Seeds from broad leafed plants often complement seeds from grasses to give the essential eight amino acids.

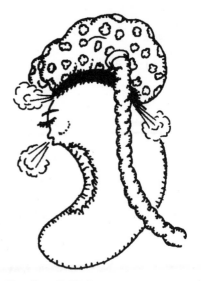

Dried Lima Beans

1 lb. dried *lima beans*
1 onion, chopped
1 C. celery, chopped
1 carrot, chopped
Water for cooking and soaking
2 garlic cloves, minced
1 t. ground *apricot kernel* or
    ground almonds. (op.)

Cover washed and sorted lima beans with water and soak overnight. The next morning cook beans until tender in large pot in same water they were soaking in. Place onion, celery, carrot, and garlic in same pot with beans to cook. When tender, place in serving bowl and sprinkle with ground kernels. Serve with corn bread. Serves four.

Minted Lima Beans

2 C. fresh *lima beans*
1½ C. water
½ t. sea salt
1 clove garlic, minced
1 T. crushed, dried mint
1 T. butter, raw

Cook beans and butter in salt water until tender, about 25 to 30 minutes. Sprinkle dried mint on top. Serves four.

Sautéed Mung Sprouts

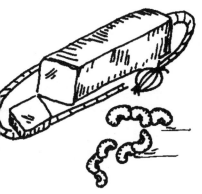

1 large onion, chopped
3 C. *mung bean sprouts*
4 t. safflower oil or sesame oil
1 stalk celery, chopped
2 t. ground *apricot kernels*

Sauté onion in oil for several minutes. Add sprouts and celery, cover skillet, and steam for four minutes. Serve with kernels sprinkled over the top. Serves four.

Sauces

Sauces help the cook in several ways. They add needed texture to dry foods, they give beautiful color and flavor to bland, colorless foods, and they give zest and excitement to the pleasure of eating.

There is no "commercial" bouillon one can purchase that begins to compare with a good home-made stock. There is no canned tomato sauce that tastes anything like a slowly simmered sauce that one makes herself.* But, you may say, "Aren't women supposed to be liberated today? And doesn't that include freedom from long hours in the kitchen?" Yes, we believe so. However, if one is home anyway, there is very little work involved in simmering a sauce.

Cooking should be creative. It can bring real happiness. We feel this is true especially when one follows the simple rules of using only natural, unprocessed foods. Then the vigorous health of one's children and husband shine forth. One can feel very proud that her time and loving care helped to make them this way. With these rewards, we feel that the time given is well worth the effort.

*Apologies to my male readers. I love you dearly, and my recipes are just as much for you too. I simply have assumed that the great bulk of my readers are women.

Mexican Spaghetti Sauce

1 lb. ground stewing beef mixed with
1 lb. ground calf heart
2 cloves garlic, minced
1 medium onion, chopped
1 small can tomato paste
1 large bell pepper, chopped
1 T. cumin
¼ C. "California Chili" powder (mild)
1 T. crushed oregano
Water

Lightly brown onion, garlic, bell pepper, and ground meat in large heavy skillet. Add spices, tomato paste, and enough water to make a medium thick sauce. Simmer about one hour, covered. Serve over *buckwheat spaghetti*. Serves six.

Almond Bechamel Sauce — White

2 T. raw butter
2 T. whole-wheat flour
1 C. half & half or raw cream
1 t. sea salt
Pinch white pepper
2 t. ground *apricot kernels*

Almond "Beurre Manie" (molded butter)

1 C. raw butter, soft
1 C. whole-wheat flour
2 t. ground *apricot kernel*s

This is simply a roux of equal parts of flour and butter and kernels blended together and then rolled into half inch balls. These are stored in a jar or plastic bag in the refrigerator until needed. One or more may be dropped into a boiling liquid to thicken it. Good for stews, soups, etc. May be used unflavored or with the almond flavoring.

Melt butter in a saucepan over moderate heat. Do not let it brown. Add flour and stir until mixture is well blended. Gradually stir in cream. Cook over medium heat, stirring constantly until mixture comes to a boil and thickens. Simmer, stirring frequently over a very low heat for 5 minutes. Season with salt, pepper, and apricot kernel to taste and add a pinch of nutmeg if desired. Serves four.

Variation: to make a velouté sauce instead, substitute hot chicken broth for the cream.

Almond Espagnole Sauce, Brown

2 T. butter
2 T. flour
1 C. beef stock (or water)
1 clove garlic, minced
Pinch of bay leaf
Pinch of parsley
Pinch of thyme
Pinch of marjoram
Pinch of allspice
1 T. tomato paste
1 T. dry white wine
2 T. *apricot kernel,* ground

Brown flour carefully in hot dry skillet (brown roux). Don't let it burn. Blend in butter. Add beef stock, herbs, tomato paste, and wine. Simmer gently until it's thick enough to coat a metal spoon. Add apricot kernels and serve over beef, veal, or lamb. Makes one cup.

Variation: add 1 T. Vinegar, 1 t. mustard, and cayenne pepper. Gives peppery flavor for kidneys, pigs' feet, liver, and veal chops.

Amandine Sauce

¼ C. ground almonds, raw
½ C. raw butter
¾ T. fresh, organic lemon
   juice
1 T. minced parsley
1 t. crushed tarragon
   leaves (op.)
1 t. *apricot kernels*, ground

Gently toast almonds in dry, hot skillet. Add butter and remaining ingredients. Heat through and remove from heat. Serve on vegetables, sweetbreads, fish, and fowl. Approx. one cup.

Buckwheat Cream Sauce

2 T. **buckwheat flour** (the "light" flour will resemble wheat flour more than the "dark" flour)

2 T. butter

1 C. milk, water, or "imitation cream", home-made

1 fertile egg (op.)

½ t. sea salt

2 T. sherry (op.)

1 T. **flax seeds** (op.)

Blend and heat the flour and butter in a saucepan over medium heat. Add the milk, all at once. Stir with wooden spoon or whisk until smooth and thick. Add a little sauce to the egg and mix thoroughly. Add the egg mixture to the sauce and stir for one minute. Don't boil again or the egg will curdle. Add remaining ingredients and use in place of wheat cream sauce in any recipe.

Cucumber Sauce

1 cucumber, thinly sliced

1 C. yogurt

1 garlic clove, minced

¼ mint leaves, chopped

2 t. ground **apricot kernels**

Mix, chill, and serve. Very good with lamb. Serves four.

Fruits

Fruit is delicious, colorful, and the pride of "mother nature." Such a fantastic array of sweetness and hue is almost beyond conception. Not only are fresh fruits luscious to the taste, but they are extremely high in essential vitamins and minerals. The wild varieties are higher in certain nutrients, however, and it would behoove us to eat these whenever possible. For example, wild choke cherries, cranberries, and crabapples are much higher in B_{17} than are the more domesticated, hybridized fruits.

Everybody needs several servings of fruit a day. Ripe fruit contains a rich supply of enzymes, minerals (if these minerals were in the growing soil), and pro-vitamin A. Eat ripe fruit grown on composted natural soils. Also eat a few of the seeds of these fruits as they contain complementary vegetable protein, poly-unsaturated oils, vitamin A, B-complex, and large amounts of vitamin E. They also provide much needed roughage. Choose intensely colored fruits, e.g. deep yellow, orange and green, for they are far richer in pro-vitamin A than their paler counterparts. For example, home grown apricots grown in rich natural soil are a much deeper color of orange than those ordinarily found in our supermarkets.

Agar-Agar

Agar-agar is a gelatinous, dried substance derived from a very special type of sea weed. It has the properties of thickening and emulsifying foods. Being a plant, it is preferred by vegetarians to the common gelatin which comes from an animal source. It is widely used by the food processing industry. It is far more effective than gelatin and will produce a dish that will never flop, for it is capable of taking up to 200 times its volume of water to make a jelly.

Agar-agar is not only useful but highly nutritious, being rich in the minerals from the ocean. It is usually made from the sea algae of the orient and is therefore sometimes called Japanese gelatin or Kanten.

When agar-agar is used, fruit and vegetable juices can be jellied merely by warming rather than by boiling, and therefore more of their health value is retained. Jellies and jams made with agar-agar rather than commercial pectin do not need nearly as much sugar or honey. Agar-agar is also useful in keeping the body "regular" for it swells to many times its bulk when it reaches the intestines and increases peristaltic action.

Agar-agar comes in flake, granulated, and bar form. These are the basic proportions to use: 3½ C. liquid to 2 T. flakes; 3½ C. liquid to 1 T. granulated; 3½ C. liquid to approximately 7″ bar form. Soak the agar-agar in 1 C. of liquid for 10 minutes, then warm on stove until dissolved; add rest of liquid, which should be at room temperature. Refrigerate if desired, but this will gel at room temperature.

Baked Apples

4 large apples, organic
Seeds from apples, ground or
  chopped
4 T. cooked **millet cereal**
1 C. water
2 C. home-made plum jam
1 t. cinnamon
½ t. nutmeg
¼ t. clove
1 T. arrowroot mixed in 3 T.
  cold water
¼ t. sea salt

Wash, core the apples ⅔ of the
way down and pare off top ⅓.
Mix millet with spices,
cinnamon, nutmeg, clove, salt,
and apple seeds. Put ¼ mixture
in center of each apple. Place
in baking dish with water.
Spoon jam over apples. Bake
for 35 minutes at 350° F.
Place apples on a serving
plate. Add arrowroot to juices
over medium heat. Stir
constantly until juice is thick
and clear. Spoon over apples
and serve. Serves four.

Raw Berry Pie

1 baked whole-wheat pie shell
8 oz. pkg. cream cheese
  softened with 1 T. milk
3 C. berries, such as
  **strawberries, raspberries,
  blackberries,
  huckleberries,** etc.
½ C. raw honey (or a little
  less)
2 C. raw cream, whipped
1 T. vanilla
½ C. shaved raw almonds,
  unblanched
1 T. **apricot kernels,** ground

Just before serving, spread
cream cheese in bottom of
cool, cooked pie shell. Fill
shell with fresh raw berries.
Drizzle honey over fruit. Whip
cream with vanilla. Pile high
on top of berries and sprinkle
almonds and kernels on top.
Serve at once. Serves six.

Apricot-Honey Jam

3½ lbs. fully ripe apricots
2 lemons, organic
1½ boxes "Sure-Jell"
5 C. honey, raw
Kernels from apricots

Pit, but do not peel, fully ripe apricots. Cut in pieces and chop fine or grind. Add ¼ C. organic lemon juice to fruit. Measure out 5 C. or 2½ lbs. of this prepared fruit. Place in 6 quart saucepan. If necessary, add water to equal 5 cups. For softer jams, use ½ C. more fruit; for stiffer jams, use ¼ C. less. Mix "Sure-Jell" with fruit in saucepan. Place over high heat and stir until mixture comes to a hard boil. Add honey all at once. Bring to a full rolling boil (a boil that cannot be stirred down). Boil hard for 2 minutes, stirring constantly. Remove from heat and skim off foam with metal spoon. Stir and skim 5 minutes to cool slightly and prevent floating fruit. Ladle into glasses, leaving half-inch space at top. Add three apricot kernels to each cup of jam. Cover jam immediately with ⅛″ hot paraffin. Cool. Cover with loose fitting lids. Store in cool dry place.

Honeyed Apples

1 t. vanilla
2 C. honey, solid
1 t. grated organic lemon rind
4½ C. thinly sliced apples with their *seeds* ground
1 t. nutmeg
1 t. cinnamon
2 t. ground *apricot kernels*

Cook honey gently for about five minutes. Stir in the vanilla and lemon rind. Gently cook the apples, a few at a time, being careful not to overcook them. Place in serving bowl with a little cooked honey poured over them. Sprinkle with a little of the mixture of nutmeg, cinnamon, and kernels. Very good with yogurt or sour cream. Serves four.

Jellied Plums

7″ bar agar-agar (see
   description, p. 134)
1 C. water
3″ cinnamon stick
2⅓ C. Burgundy wine
½ C. *sorghum cane syrup*
2 C. plum halves, including
   skins and *kernels*

Break agar-agar into pieces
and soak in cup of water.
Place in saucepan over
medium heat. Add cinnamon
and heat gently until dissolved
(about 20 minutes). Remove
from heat, take out the
cinnamon stick, add wine,
syrup, and mix well.
Refrigerate until partially
jelled. Add the plums and
return to refrigerator to
complete jelling. Serves six.

Plum Honey Jam

3 lbs. fully ripe plums
1½ boxes "Sure-Jell"
6 C. raw honey
Kernels from plums

Pit, but do not peel plums.
Chop fine. Add ½ C. water.
Simmer, covered for 5 minutes.
This is done by bringing the
fruit to a boil, reducing heat,
covering and cooking gently
for 5 minutes. Measure out 6
C. or 3 pounds of cooked fruit.
Place in 6 to 8 quart saucepan.
If necessary, add water to
equal this amount. For softer
jams, use ½ C. more fruit; for
stiffer jams, use ¼ C. less. Mix
"Sure-Jell" with fruit in
saucepan. Place over high heat
and stir until mixture comes to
a hard boil. Add honey at
once. Bring to a full rolling
boil, a boil that cannot be
stirred down. Boil hard for 2
minutes, stirring constantly.
Remove from heat and skim
off foam with metal spoon.
Stir and skim for 5 minutes.
Ladle into glasses, leaving a
half-inch space at top. Add
four plum kernels to each cup
of jam. Cover jam immediately
with ⅛″ paraffin. Cool and
cover with loose-fitting lids.
Store in cool dry place.

Peaches Melba

2 fresh peaches
1 T. honey
1 T. slivered unblanched raw
   almonds
1 C. *raspberries*
1 pint home-made almond or
   vanilla ice cream
1 T. honey
Kernels from peaches

Poach peaches in boiling
water for one minute. Remove
to bowl. Peel and halve
peaches. Crack stones and
grind kernels. Set aside. Put
honey on peaches and sprinkle
with seeds. Chill in refrigerator for one hour. Rub or mash
raspberries to a pulp. Don't
remove raspberry seeds. Stir
in 1 T. honey.

To assemble, place a scoop of
ice cream in each of four
bowls or goblets. Place peach
half on top with dome side up.
Next, pour raspberries over
this and, lastly, sprinkle slivered almonds. Serve at once.

Cherries Jubilee

3 C. fresh bing cherries, crack
   pits, save the **kernels**
½ C. gin
¼ C. raw honey
Cherry kernels, ground
Home-made vanilla ice cream
   or home-made "imitation"

Remove cherry pits with
button hook or large hairpin,
being careful not to crush
cherries. Place cherries in cold
skillet (not aluminum). Add
honey and heat carefully until
cherries begin to lose juice
and are heated through. Add
ground cherry kernels and stir
in. Heat to simmer. Add the
gin, stand back, and touch
liquid surface with long
lighted match. Serve flaming
over ice cream.

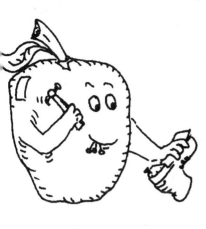

Crisp Apple Cobbler

4 C. sliced apples, organic, unpeeled, save the seeds
⅝ C. *sorghum cane syrup*
Mix together a dash of each of the following: mace, clove, nutmeg, cinnamon, allspice
½ C. raisins, unsulfured
½ C. dark-brown sugar
¼ t. sea salt
½ C. cold butter, raw
⅔ C. raw pecans, chopped
Ground *seeds* from apples

Place apples and raisins in shallow baking dish. Pour syrup over them. Mix together the spices, sugar, salt, and flour. Manually blend in the cold butter to a crumb consistency. Sprinkle over the apples and bake in a 350° F. oven for about 30 minutes. Sprinkle apple seeds and pecans on top. Serve. Serves four.

Fruit Filled Watermelon

Cut thin horizontal slice from bottom of watermelon so it will rest evenly. Slice watermelon lengthwise in half. Carve a decorative zigzag edge from sliced edge. Scoop out fruit to form a bowl. Scoop melon balls from second half.

Fill bowl with watermelon balls and other melon balls, or several of the following: *boysenberries, loganberries, quince*, peaches, plums, apricots, cherries, *red* and *black raspberries, blackberries, huckleberries*, *strawberries*, blueberries or pineapple chunks.

Apple Crisp

1 C. sifted whole-wheat pastry flour (or *buckwheat flour*)
3 ozs. cream cheese (or thick yogurt)
3 red apples and their *seeds*, finely chopped
8 T. raw butter
2 T. unsulfured raisins
2 t. ground *apricot kernels*
Pinch sea salt
½ C. dark-brown sugar
1½ t. cinnamon
2 T. butter, raw
Spicy Sauce*

Cream flour, salt, cream cheese, and butter together quickly. Chill. Roll into rectangle about 8″ x 15″. Spread with apricot kernels, apples, sugar, and cinnamon. Roll up like a jelly roll and cut into 1¼″ slices. The easiest way to cut them is to wrap a string once around the roll at the place to be cut, then sharply pull the ends of the string tightly together. Place slices 1″ apart in rectangular baking dish. Cover with Spicy Sauce and bake in 400° F. oven for 12 minutes, and then turn oven down for 45 minutes to 325°F. Serves four.

*Spicy Sauce: Mix
½ C. brown sugar
1 C. water
2 T. whole-wheat flour
1 T. raw butter
1¼ t. cinnamon
½ t. nutmeg
1 t. allspice, and
1 T. vanilla.

Cook until clear and thick.

Applesauce

5 C. tart apples, peeled, cored, and chopped (peeling op.)
Seeds from apples, ground
1 C. raw honey
1 t. nutmeg
¼ C. raisins, light, organic (op.)

Place all ingredients in saucepan. Stir until the honey has dissolved. Cover and cook gently for about 20 minutes. Very good served over cooked millet cereal or with yogurt. Serves four.

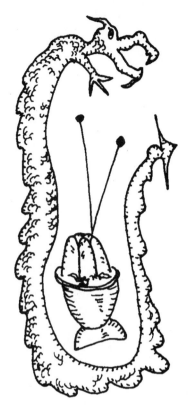

Fruit Gelatin, Oriental Style Vegetarian

7″ stick of Kanten or
    agar-agar
1 C. water
2 C. mixed fruit, chopped
    (include berries*, drupes†,
    and their **kernels**, ground)
⅓ C. raw honey
½ C. almond milk, raw,
    "imitation cream,"
    home-made or commercial
    yogurt, thinned (see index)
¼ t. **apricot kernels,** ground
⅔ C. raw honey
½ C. water
2 t. organic lemon juice
2 t. grated lemon rind, organic

Wash and wring out Kanten. Place the Kanten in 1 C. water and heat. After Kanten dissolves, add ⅓ C. honey, almond milk, and kernels. Chill to harden. Mix honey and water. Add the lemon juice, fruit, rind, and chilled Kanten, cut into cubes. Pour mixture into a wet mold and chill. Serves four.

*Berries such as **strawberries**, **raspberries**, and **blackberries**, etc.

† Drupes are fruits with a center stone such as peaches, plums and cherries.

"Pickled" Berries

4 C. solid "creamed" honey
4 C. berries, raw organic, such
    as **raspberries**,
    blackberries, etc.
½ C. apple cider vinegar
½ t. allspice
½ t. cinnamon
½ t. cloves
Pinch nutmeg
1 package dry pectin

Mix all ingredients together except pectin. Cook at high boil for one minute. Remove from heat and add pectin. Mix well. Pack in sterile jars. Seal. Eight cups.

Mr. Lindy's Fruit and Yogurt

1 unpeeled pear & *seeds*,* cut up
1 unpeeled apple and its *seeds*,* cut up
3 apricots and their *kernels*,* cup up
3 plums and their *seeds*,* cut up
1 banana, cut up
¼ C. fresh pineapple, cut up
½ C. plum purée
½ C. home-made plum juice

Mix fruits and ground seeds and place into bowls. Scoop yogurt (preferably home-made from raw, whole milk) on top of mixed fruit. Ladle purée on top of yogurt and pour juice over all.
*Grind seeds and kernels in blender.

Cranberry Nut Parfait

1 C. frozen *cranberries*, raw
½ C. raw honey
2 fertile eggs, separated
2 t. *apricot kernels,* ground
1 C. home-made cream, non-dairy

Blend all of the ingredients in blender at high speed. Fold in egg whites. Pour into freezing tray and freeze four hours.

Raw Apple Sauce

6 large apples, organic, chopped coarsely (don't peel, save seeds)
1 large organic orange, peeled, seeded and coarsely chopped
½ C. organic apple juice
1 T. organic lemon juice
1 t. cinnamon
1 t. nutmeg
1 t. sea salt
1 t. vanilla extract
Seeds from the apples

Blend apples and seeds with apple juice at high speed. Add the orange and blend again. Add remaining ingredients and serve. Serves four.

Strawberries Chantilly

1 C. crushed *strawberries*
1 T. raw honey
1 C. raw cream, whipped
1 t. vanilla
2 C. home-made coconut ice cream
½ C. ground raw almonds
1 t. *apricot kernels,* ground

Mix honey into strawberries. Place ice cream equally in four sherbert glasses or goblets. Add vanilla to whipped cream. Place this on top of the ice cream. Place the strawberries on top of the whipped cream and sprinkle the almonds and kernels over this. Serve at once. Serves four.

Apple Butter

5 C. tart organic apples with their *seeds*
2½ C. organic apple juice
Sorghum cane syrup, or creamed honey
4 t. cinnamon
2 t. nutmeg
¾ t. cloves

Core and chop apples. Grind the seeds. Blend together. For each cup of pulp add ⅓ C. creamed or solid honey, or syrup. Add spices and cook over medium heat, stirring constantly until mixture sheets from a spoon. Pour in sterile jars and seal with paraffin. Approximately two quarts.

Strawberry Cream

2 C. *strawberries*, fresh
2 C. yogurt, unflavored
¼ C. raw honey
2 t. *apricot kernels,* ground

Whirl in blender and serve. Raspberries or other berries may be substituted. A raw egg may be added. Serves four.

Fruit Compote

Fresh mint
½ C. May wine or white wine
    and ½ T. woodruff*
    soaked in wine overnight
1 C. each of any three soft
    fresh fruits and their *seeds*.
1 orange and rind, organic
1 lemon and rind, organic

Cut up peeled orange and
place in a large bowl. Add
other fruits, such as raspberries,
cherries, apricots, peaches,
plums, blueberries, etc.,
including their de-pitted and
ground seeds. Sprinkle grated
rinds and May wine over fruit.
Mix in mint and chill. Serve
alone in punch bowl, over
cake, or with cookies, etc.
Serves four.

Variation: non-alcoholic fruit
compote can be made by
substituting fruit juice mixed
with a little honey and lemon
juice for the wine.

*Woodruff is an herb.

Blackberry Sherbert

10 oz. frozen *blackberries*
    (loose pack)
½ C. *sorghum cane syrup*
¾ C. raw milk (or yogurt)
½ tray small ice cubes made
    with spring water

Put syrup and milk in blender.
Blend at high speed. Add fruit.
Blend. Add ice, blending a
few cubes at a time. May be
served as a slush or frozen.
Any other berries, fresh or
frozen, may be substituted.
Serves four.

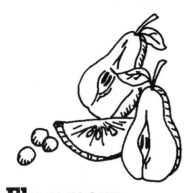

Flummery

2 C. *berries*
2 C. water
3 T. arrowroot
½ C. *sorghum cane syrup*
1 t. sea salt

Simmer berries for 10 minutes. Blackberries, blueberries, strawberries or raspberries are all good. Blend the arrowroot with the cold water and stir into the cooking berries. Stir until smooth, thick, and clear. Blend in the syrup. Chill. Very good with cream or over cake or custard. Serves four.

Rumtopf

3 organic oranges, peeled and chopped
2 fresh, organic pears, cored and chopped
1¼ C. *cranberries*
½ C. *blackberries*
1 C. honey, raw
1 C. rum
Any fruit may be added (include their seeds)

Combine all ingredients. Place in crock. Cover lightly and refrigerate for two weeks. For every cup of fruit removed add one cup fruit, ¼ C. honey and ¼ C. rum. Serves four.

Fruit Ices

Place one tray of ice cubes, made with clear spring water, in blender with just enough water to lift and float the ice cubes. Blend at high speed to make "ice snow." Blend in 10 ounces of fresh or frozen loose-pack berries such as *strawberries*, *blackberries*, *red* or *black raspberries*, *huckleberries, gooseberries, loganberries, boysenberries,* or *quince.* Add ¼ C. honey and blend again. Serve in cups or freeze.

Plum Juice and Plum Purée

10 lbs. Santa Rosa plums
(20 C.) ripe fruit only
Seeds from the plums
2½ C. raw honey

Remove pits from the plums. Wear rubber gloves to prevent stained fingers, and squeeze pits out with your fingers. Put four cups of pitted plums in blender and add ½ cup honey. Blend at high speed for about 45 seconds or until pulp and peel are ground to a purée. Pour into 1 qt. mason jars. Continue same process until all fruit is blended and contained. Place jars in refrigerator for 3 to 5 days. A very thick purée will be in upper half of jar and a beautifully clear and dark red juice will be in the bottom half. The purée should be skimmed off the top and frozen. This can be placed in freezer bags and freezer boxes. The juice at the bottom can be collected in a ½ gallon jug and stored in the refrigerator or in heavy freezer bags and also frozen.

The juice is quite concentrated and is good diluted 1:1 with organic, unsweetened apple juice.

*Suggestion: Break open a few pits and grind kernels. Add about ¼ t. ground seed to each cup purée or juice. Makes 5 quarts.

*This recipe works well for all "drupe" fruit (fruit with a single, central pit).

Apple Nut Filling for Sandwiches

1 large finely chopped,
organic, unpeeled apple
Seeds from apple, ground
1 t. fennel or anise seed
1 T. raw ground walnuts
8 oz. cream cheese (or thick
yogurt)
Cream (or apple juice) to
moisten

Mix all ingredients together. Chill. Spread on whole-wheat bread with **watercress** sprigs.

Orange Freeze

1 medium sized can of frozen, unsweetened orange juice
1 medium sized apple, cored and coarsely chopped
Seeds from apple
1 tray medium to small sized ice cubes

Place orange juice in the blender. Start blender. Add the apple and the seeds. Blend at high speed. Add a few ice cubes at a time until thoroughly blended. Serve in paper cups. Any frozen, unsweetened juice concentrate may be used. Serves four.

Pink Fluff Dressing

1 C. sour cream
3 T. *raspberry* or plum purée
1 T. *sorghum cane syrup*

Mix and chill. Serve with fruit. Serves four.

Dairy Products

There is, at the present time, a controversy over milk. Is it or isn't it good for adults to drink milk? Speaking personally, your author has observed good physical results from the consumption of at least one cup of milk a day. I feel that it is the most reliable source of calcium in the American diet. Calcium is a mineral that not only is needed for the construction of and continued replacement in bones and teeth, but also is a requirement for muscle action, good eye-sight, and clear skin. There are, of course, other less reliable sources of calcium such as very green vegetables, including chard and parsley. Another source is dark unsulfured molasses.

Some people do not have the enzyme lactase for the digestion of milk sugar. For these people we heartily recommend the cultured milks. These milks, having already had their lactose converted to lactic acid, are easily digested.

I feel that it's about time we all tapered off of the high consumption of powdered milk. This milk, even the spray-dried, is "cooked." It is also high in artificial vitamin D *and quite often high in strontium [90].* Needless to say, a little of this goes a long way, and a cup or two a day could be toxic. An unsuspected source of highly concentrated powdered milk is in the "protein" powders and tablets so popular today.

I recommend whole milk, including the cream. The cream is high in vitamin A and is needed for calcium metabolism. I also recommend "living" or certified raw milk whenever possible. Cooking or pasteurizing milk destroys vitamins and enzymes and alters some of the protein. **

Cultured Raw Milks

(Free of Powdered Milk)

There are three major milk cultures used in America today. They are:

> buttermilk
> kefir
> yogurt

You can use any or all of these foods to make your own cultures. Your own cultures will be superior because they will have all the advantages of raw milk and lactic acid too.

1. **"Thick Milk:"** Inoculate two cups of certified raw milk with ¼ C. buttermilk. Cover container and set on side board for 24 hours. The resulting custard is very mildly sour. Be sure to eat

---

*Hunter, Beatrice T.; *Consumer Beware*, pg 224–254
**Bellew, Bernard; *Diet Dynamics,* pg 82–83

both the curds and whey. The whey is high in calcium. You may always use some of the current "thick milk" to inoculate a new batch. Any mold that might form is harmless. Scrape it off or eat it. This mold is useful in the making of cheese and it is delicious.

2. **Kefir:** Inoculate 2 cups certified raw milk with ¼ C. unflavored kefir. Cover container and set on side board for 48 hours. The resulting custard is medium sour. A very tasty and nutritious drink can be made by mixing in the blender this kefir culture and fruit juices, fresh fruit or frozen fruit. Honey or sorghum cane syrup may be used to sweeten.

3. **Yogurt**: Add 2 cups certified raw milk to ¼ C. unflavored commercial yogurt. Cover container and set on sideboard for 72 hours. The resulting custard is quite sour. This is good because pathogenic bacteria do not live in lactic acid, and if you have a gastro-intestinal problem, the more sour it is, the more helpful it is. Most people don't like yogurt "straight" because of its sourness. However, they will find that it tastes quite sweet when served with fresh fruit (especially Thompson's seedless grapes). Another favorite is to pour sorghum cane syrup, honey, or genuine maple syrup over the yogurt, sundae fashion. We like peach or plum purée, sweetened with honey, poured over a bowlful, and the top sprinkled with ground peach kernels. It also can be mixed into a fruit drink or used in place of cream to make a sort of "mushy" ice cream.

Berta's Almond Cream Non-Dairy

Place all the ingredients in the blender and blend at high speed. May be used over cereal, in decaffeinated drinks, etc. Three cups.

1½ C. almonds, raw, ground
1 t. *apricot kernels,* ground
1½ C. water
¼ t. ground *flax seeds*
2 t. honey, raw (for a darker cream use **sorghum cane syrup**)
1 t. vanilla extract

Yogurt

⅓ C. yogurt, commercial, unflavored
3½ C. certified raw milk (or whole pasteurized milk, scalded)

Mix ingredients together in blender. Pour into qt. jar. Lightly cover jar. Wrap in wool scarf and put in warm place. Curd will form in 8 hours if kept at about 110° F. The best way to do this is to put wrapped yogurt in styrofoam picnic basket with a jar of hot water. Keep basket cover sealed tightly and change water in jar when it becomes cool. Or keep yogurt in warm cozy place on counter or closet. It will curd in about 72 hours. One quart.

Yogurt is very good served chilled with ground raw *macadamia* or *Brazil nuts* and/or raw apricots, plums and peaches sliced on top.

A few milk recipes also are contained in the following section on beverages.

Imitation Cream Non-Dairy

¼ C. *millet* ground, dry

Add to: 1 C. cold water and ¼ t. sea salt in saucepan. Bring to boil. Stir constantly until thick and smooth.

Then add: 1 C. water
4 T. safflower oil
1 fertile egg yolk

Mix in blender and chill. Strain and serve over cereals. Suggested for "imitation" coffee, baking, cooking, etc.

Raw Cottage Cheese

2 qts. certified raw milk, soured or sweet
½ C. buttermilk or yogurt
Sea salt to taste
Sprinkle *apricot kernels*

Place milk in large container. Stir in the culture. Cover and set aside at room temperature for 24 hours. Strain in cheese cloth. Lightly salt, add the kernels, and serve. Save whey for soup, sauce, etc. or feed to loving and grateful plants.

Beverages

Beverages can be thirst quenching, refreshing, and also nourishing. Instead of serving soda-pop to your family, buy 100% fruit juices, pour over ice into tall frosty glasses, and top with mint sprigs or home-made ice cream. Make sodas by adding sparkling water or spring water to carob milk and topping with

153

home-made ice cream. Puréed fruits diluted with sparkling water and a squeeze of lime are refreshing. Ice cold vegetable juices also are good especially when mixed with fruit juices. For example, beet juice with boysenberry or strawberry juice; celery and/or spinach juice with pineapple juice; and carrot juice with coconut or almond milk and a pinch of ground apricot kernel are delightful.

Wine with Fresh Fruit

Small bottle white wine,
    champagne, or club soda
    and apple juice
4 small peaches, peeled and
    chilled with a little honey
4 sprigs mint
2 t. ground peach or apricot
    kernels

Prick peaches and place in
champagne glasses. Add wine
or juice. Decorate with mint
and serve, sprinkled with
kernels. For red wine or a red
juice such as boysenberry
juice, do the same thing with a
large strawberry.

Hercules Milk (High Protein Drink) Complete B-complex

1 quart certified raw milk (or
    water*)
½ C. yeast powder, inactive
½ C. toasted or freshly ground
    raw wheat germ
¼ C. unhulled sesame seeds
¼ C. chia seeds
1 T. powdered lecithin
2 T. calcium gluconate or
    1 T. calcium lactate
1 C. yogurt
½ C. *sorghum cane syrup*
¼ t. magnesium oxide powder
¼ C. safflower oil
2 t. *apricot kernels,* ground
1 t. raw liver powder (op.)

Mix in the blender at high
speed. Serve. This makes
1½ quarts which contains 115
grams of protein and
approximately 2500 calories.
Each 8 oz. glass contains 20
grams protein and 415 calories.

*For low milk diets

B$_{17}$ Cocktails

-1-

2 C. *watercress*, firmly
    pressed
2 C. unsweetened pineapple
    juice
1 t. *apricot kernels,* ground
6 ice cubes
4 sprigs mint
Liquify one minute in the
blender. Pour into frosty
glasses and serve.

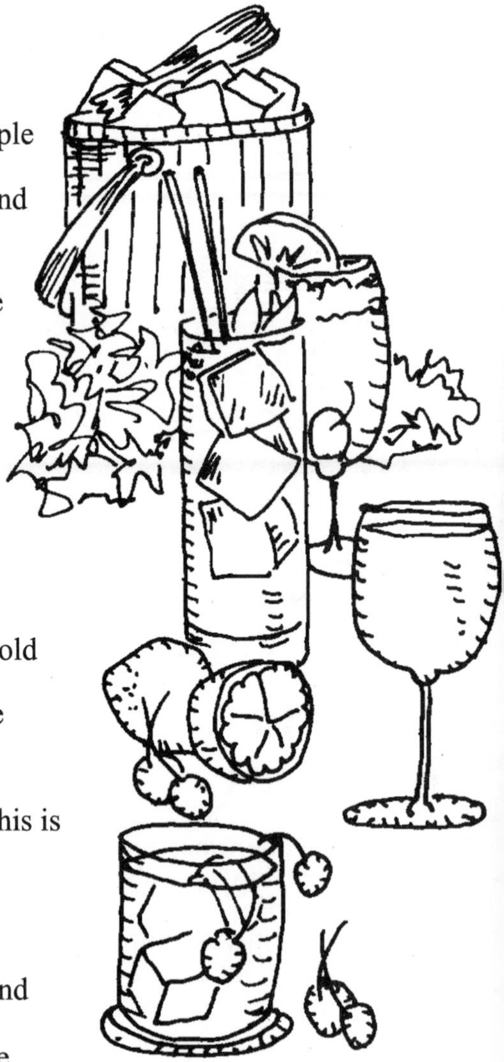

-2-

1 C. *alfalfa sprouts*
1 C. raw apple juice
10 *apple seeds*
12 raw almonds
4 sprigs parsley
4 sprigs mint
6 ice cubes and enough cold
    water to thin a little.
Liquify one minute in the
blender and serve.

-3-

3 T. soya-milk powder (this is
    cooked soy flour)
6 raw almonds
2 T. carob powder
2 t. *sorghum cane syrup*
1 t. *apricot kernels,* ground
2 C. carrot juice
Liquify in blender for one
minute. Serve in chilled
glasses.

-4-

2 C. organic apple juice, raw
10 *apple seeds*
2 C. *cranberries*, raw
6 ice cubes
Blend for two minutes and
serve.

-5-

2 C. papaya juice
⅔ C. apricots dried, unsulfured
½ C. pineapple juice
¼ C. *sorghum cane syrup*
1 t. *apricot kernels*, ground
6 ice cubes
Liquify in blender for two
minutes and serve. Serves two.

Fruit-Nog

2 fertile eggs
⅔ C. raw honey or *sorghum cane syrup*
½ C. safflower oil
1 t. vanilla extract
1 C. ice (Shaved if blender won't grind it.)
2 C. *boysenberries, blackberries, strawberries, raspberries,* or *huckleberries*
1 T. gelatin (1 envelope)*
½ C. water

Soften gelatin in water. Place remaining ingredients in blender. Blend at high speed until well blended (about 1 minute). Add the softened gelatin and continue blending until smooth. Pour into glasses and serve.

*Gelatin can be a very good and inexpensive source of protein. The only problem is, it only has six of the eight essential amino acids. So, just as with all incomplete proteins, the body rejects the substance *as a protein*. It may be utilized for other benefits, but it will not prevent "kwashiorkor," i.e. protein deficiency disease. If, however, an incomplete protein such as gelatin, grains, beans, legumes, etc. is served with a complete protein, such as eggs, the body accepts and utilizes it as complete protein.

Sharon's Egg Nog

2 C. raw milk, chilled
2 fertile eggs
1 banana
1 t. s*orghum cane syrup*
2 T. carob powder
1 t. inactive yeast powder, primary or brewers'
2 T. raw wheat germ, fresh
2 T. powdered milk, non-instant
2 t. *apricot kernels,* ground

Blend all the ingredients together in the blender at high speed. Drink at once. Contains about 35 grams of complete protein.

Carob Millet Shake, Non-Dairy

3 fertile eggs, soft boiled
1 C. cooked ground *millet cereal*
⅔ C. water
1 T. *flax seeds*
⅔ C. almond oil
4 T. raw honey
4 T. carob
1 T. vanilla
1 tray ice cubes

Grind flax seeds to a powder in the blender. Add water and blend at high speed. Add the remaining ingredients and continue blending. Add a few ice cubes at a time. When thick and creamy, may be eaten or put in paper cups and frozen.

Sister's "Mug O'Superman"

1 C. *raspberries*, fresh
½ C. raw chicken liver, organic
1 T. honey
½ ripe banana

Grind liver in the blender until liquefied. Strain thoroughly. Replace liquefied liver in the blender with the rest of the ingredients. Blend thoroughly and serve. (If you don't tell him it's liver, he'll never know!) Serves one.

Almond Egg Nog

2 eggs, fresh, fertile
2 oz. raw cream (or home-made "imitation cream")
1 T. *sorghum cane syrup*
1 t. vanilla
½ t. ground *apricot kernels*

Blend at high speed for about 30 seconds in blender. Best if all ingredients are chilled. High in vitamin A and E. High in choline, inositol, biotin, lecithin, riboflavin, B_{17}, iron and other minerals. This makes a quick nourishing breakfast for a nominal cost. About 350 calories. It is very filling and so satisfying. You shouldn't be hungry again 'til lunch time. Serves one.

Cranberry Punch

2 qts. unfiltered, organic apple juice
4 C. *cranberry* juice
1 C. *cranberry* sauce, home-made
4 C. carbonated water
1 organic lemon, sliced thinly
1 organic lime, sliced thinly
3 t. ground *apricot kernels*

Chill first three ingredients together, chill last three ingredients separately. Just before serving, combine all ingredients in punch bowl, allowing the lemon and lime to float. May add small block of ice. Serves twelve.

Peach Juice and Peach Purée

7 lbs. peaches, peeled (20 C.), ripe fruit only
Kernels from the peaches
2½ C. raw honey

Remove pits from the peaches. Wear rubber gloves to prevent stained fingers, and squeeze pits out with your fingers. Put four cups of pitted peaches in blender and add ½ cup honey. Blend at high speed for about 45 seconds or until pulp is ground to a purée. Pour into 1 qt. mason jars. Continue same process until all fruit is blended and contained. Place jars in refrigerator for 3 to 5 days. A very thick purée will be in upper half of jar and a beautifully clear juice will be in the bottom half. The purée should be skimmed off the top and frozen. This can be placed in freezer bags and freezer boxes. The juice at the bottom can be collected in a ½ gallon jug and stored in the refrigerator or in heavy freezer bags and also frozen. The juice is quite concentrated and is good diluted 1:1 with organic, unsweetened apple juice.

*Suggestion: Break open a few pits and grind kernels. Add about ¼ t. ground seed to each cup purée or juice. Five quarts.

*This recipe works well for a "drupe" fruit (fruit with a single, central pit).

Grape Freeze

1 med. sized can of frozen, unsweetened grape juice
1 med sized apple, organic, cored and coarsely chopped
Seeds from apple
1 tray medium to small sized ice cubes

Place grape juice in the blender. Start blender. Add the apple and the seeds. Blend at high speed. Add a few ice cubes at a time until thoroughly blended. Serve in paper cups. Any frozen, unsweetened juice concentrate may be used. Serves four.

Desserts

Unfortunately the typical American diet includes a "gooey" sweet dish at the end of each meal. If your family insists on this "treat," we suggest that it be as nourishing as the rest of the fare. This is not hard to do if one is a little "sneaky." Replace present ingredients with unrefined foodstuffs. Use only whole-wheat

161

flour, honey, or sorghum cane syrup, natural extracts and, above all, don't use alkalizers, such as baking powder or bicarbonate of soda. These neutralize stomach acids and partially destroy the B-complex vitamins.

Raw fruit and/or natural raw cheese are delicious when served for dessert. Chilled raw fruit, sprinkled with ground nut kernels and served with sour cream, is very satisfying. Baked custard or a rich custard sauce served over a chilled fruit compote is also enjoyable.

For health's sake avoid using hard or hydrogenated fats or artificial colors. Don't cook your fruit. You "kill" it and cheat yourself out of valuable enzymes. Eat fruit raw.

Also see Fruit section for delicious fruit desserts.

Scotch Short-Bread Cookies

1 C. raw butter
10 T. raw solid honey (Spun Honey or other)
2½ C. whole-wheat pastry flour, sifted
1 T. vanilla
2 t. **apricot kernels,** ground
½ C. grated raw unsweetened coconut

Whip the butter until smooth and creamy. Blend in the honey and then the remaining ingredients. Drop by spoonfuls onto buttered cookie sheet 1″ apart. Bake at 350° F. for about 15 minutes. These make Spritz cookies when cookie gun is used. Three dozen.

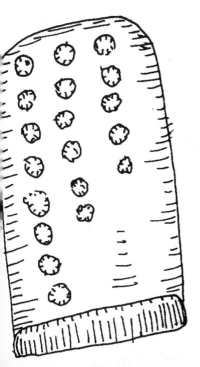

Almond Crumbles

1 C. raw butter cold
1 C. dark-brown sugar
2½ C. whole-wheat pastry flour
2 fertile eggs, separated
1 t. vanilla
½ t. sea salt
1 C. ground raw almonds
1 T. ground **apricot kernels**

Using finger tips, blend the sugar, flour, and almonds into the cold, hard butter quickly. Add the egg yolks, vanilla, and salt. Form into 1″ balls (may have to squeeze tightly). Dip in unbeaten egg whites. Flatten slightly and place on greased cookie sheet. Bake at 360° F. for 15 minutes. 48 cookies.

Rich Custard Sauce

½ C. **sorghum cane syrup** or honey
¼ t. sea salt
12 fertile egg yolks or 6 whole eggs
4 C. milk, raw
1 T. vanilla extract
1 T. **apricot kernels,** ground

Mix the first four ingredients in the blender. Pour into stainless steel or glass pan and heat to 175° F., stirring constantly. Remove from heat. Chill. Mix in the vanilla and apricot kernels. Serve over slices of Almond White Cake or raw fruit compote. Serves six.

Caren's German Nut Cake

12 fertile eggs, separated
2 C. dark-brown sugar
2 C. ground, raw nuts, hazelnuts, almonds etc.
1 T. ground **apricot kernels**

Beat egg yolks with sugar until very thick. Grind nuts and kernels in blender until dry (like coarse flour), but not too long as the nuts become "sticky." Beat whites until stiff. Fold in carefully. Keep at it. This takes a while. Pour into greased tube pan. Bake 1 hour at 325° F. When done, allow to cool slightly and remove from pan. Invert and frost with light honey frosting or eat unfrosted with fresh berries.

Pink Mallow Fluff

1 C. frozen *cranberries*
½ C. cold water
½ C. boiling water
½ C. unrefined, almond oil
2 t. ground *apricot kernels*
¾ C. raw honey
2 T. gelatin

Soften the gelatin in a blender with cold water. Blend for several minutes. Then add the boiling water, oil, apricot kernels, and honey. When thoroughly blended, add the frozen cranberries. Pour in bowl and chill. Serves four.

Almond Rounds

2 C. pastry whole-wheat flour
¼ C. dark-brown sugar
½ t. sea salt
2 C. finely chopped raw
    almonds
2 t. ground *apricot kernels*
1 C. finely ground raw
    almonds
1 C. raw butter
2 t. vanilla

Sift together flour and sugar. Add salt and sift again. Work in butter and vanilla. Add finely chopped almonds and apricot kernels. Mix well. Form into small balls, about 1″ diameter. Roll in finely ground almonds. Bake on ungreased cookie sheet at 325° F., until lightly browned —about 25 minutes. Cool on wire rack. Approx. 4 dozen.

Torbenbaden

5 fertile eggs, separated
1 C. dark-brown sugar
1 organic grated lemon rind
    and juice
1½ C. whole-wheat pastry
    flour
1½ t. grated *apricot kernels*

Separate eggs. Beat whites until stiff. Cream yolks with lemon rind, juice, and sugar. Fold egg whites into egg yolks. Then, lightly fold flour and apricot kernels into mixture. Pour into ungreased tube pan. Bake at 350° F. for about 30 minutes. Test by inserting straw or silver knife into cake. When it comes out "clean," cake is done. When cool, serve with fresh berries (strawberries, raspberries or blackberries) and whipped cream. Serves six.

Almond White Sponge Cake

1 C. sifted whole-wheat pastry
    flour or light *buckwheat*
    flour
2 C. honey or s*orghum cane*
    syrup
1½ C. fertile egg whites (about
    12 eggs), stiffly beaten
½ t. sea salt
1 t. vanilla
1 T. ground *apricot kernels*

Place honey in a saucepan and cook over medium heat until it reaches a temperature of 240° F. or the soft ball stage. Beat egg whites until very stiff. Slowly drizzle the warm honey in as you continue to beat the egg whites. Fold in the flour very carefully so as not to disturb the air in the whites. Fold in remaining ingredients. Pour into 9″ ungreased tube pan and bake in a 325° F. oven for about an hour. Invert until cool. Frost with Almond Frosting. Use egg yolks to make custard to serve on side. Serves six.

Home-Made Mince Meat

1 organic orange, ground
1 organic lemon, ground
2½ C. unsulfured raisins (part may be *currants*)
3 lbs. apples, finely chopped, including *seeds* (may be re-hydrated dried organic apples)
3 C. *sorghum cane syrup*
⅓ C. apple cider vinegar
1½ t. sea salt
1½ t. each: cinnamon, cloves, nutmeg
2 T. minced cooked beef or boiled hamburger (op.)
9″ unbaked pie shell and lattice top

Mix in order. Place in a heavy kettle and simmer until thick, about 25 minutes. Pour slightly cooled mixture into cold shell. Quickly place lattice on top. Bake in hot oven (450° F.) for 15 to 20 minutes or until crust is brown. Beaten egg may be brushed on top of crust before baking. Cool and serve. Enough for a 9″ pie.

Yam Pie (crustless)

1 T. gelatin
¼ C. apple juice, organic
½ C. raw milk (or yogurt)
1¼ C. mashed, cooked *yams*
3 T. *sorghum cane syrup*
¼ T. sea salt
½ t. nutmeg
1 t. cinnamon
½ t. ginger
3 eggs, fertile, separated

Dissolve the gelatin in the juice. Mix into hot milk. Add the yams, syrup, salt, nutmeg, cinnamon, and ginger. Cook gently in double boiler until thick. Cool to lukewarm. Stir in the egg yolks. Cool until set. Beat with mixer. Fold in stiffly beaten egg whites. Pour into pie dish and chill until firm. Serves four.

Almond Bavarian Cream

2 envelopes (2 T.) gelatin
softened in
½ C. cold milk in blender.
Add ⅓ C. boiling water and
start blender.
Add ½ C. honey
4 organic, fertile eggs
1 T. vanilla
2 t. grated *apricot kernels*
½ C. raw cream (or "imitation
cream" and/or almond
cream) and enough milk to
make 4 C. liquid.
Pour into mold and chill.
Will also need unroasted
almonds.

Chill four hours or preferably
overnight. Slightly warm the
exterior of the mold with a hot
towel and place upside down
on a serving plate. Decorate
with unroasted almonds.
Serves four.

Coconut Custard Pie, Non-Dairy

4 large, fertile eggs
2 C. home-made "imitation
cream"
½ C. *sorghum cane syrup*
1 T. vanilla extract
1 t. nutmeg
½ C. unsweetened, grated
coconut
1 baked *buckwheat* crust

Mix all of the ingredients,
except the coconut, in the
blender at high speed. Pour
into baked pie crust. Sprinkle
the coconut over the top and
bake at 300° F. until done.
This takes about 45 minutes.
Test by inserting silver knife.
When it comes out clean
instead of "gooey" the pie is
done. Serve hot or chilled.
Makes a 9″ pie.

Yellow Sponge Cake

1½ C. fertile egg whites, beaten (approx. 9 eggs)
¼ t. sea salt
1 C. honey
1½ C. whole-wheat, pastry flour, or light *buckwheat* flour
9 egg yolks, beaten (save three for frosting)
1 T. grated organic orange rind or 2 t. grated *apricot kernels*
1 t. vanilla extract

Beat the egg whites until very stiff. Slowly drizzle in the honey while continuing to beat. Fold in the flour and salt then the yolks and flavorings. Bake in a tube pan, ungreased, for about 1¼ hours at a temperature of 325° F. Invert pan until cool. Remove and frost with Buttercup Frosting. Serves six.

Pumpkin or Sweet Potato Pie

2 fertile eggs, beaten
1¾ C. pumpkin or *sweet potato* pulp
2 T. *sorghum cane syrup*
½ t. sea salt
1¼ t. cinnamon
¾ t. ginger
½ t. cloves
1⅔ C. whipping cream
1 9″ unbaked pie shell, whole-wheat (or *buckwheat*)

Mix in order. Bake in hot oven (425° F.) for 15 minutes. Reduce to 350° F. and bake for 45 minutes or until a silver knife slips out clean. Cool, then chill. Serve with whipped cream mixed with a little ground apricot kernel if desired. Serves six.

Wheat-Free Pie Crust

3 C. *buckwheat flour*
2 small fertile eggs
⅔ C. soy or corn oil
2 T. fresh organic lemon juice
2–4 T. ice water
½ t. sea salt

Place flour in bowl. Mix the eggs, oil, and juice in blender at high speed. Pour over flour and blend with fingers until a crumb-like texture is achieved. Pour the water over the flour, a little at a time, until dough holds a shape when it's squeezed in your hand. Press firmly into pie plate. Bake at 425° F. until brown, about 20 minutes. Cool and fill with corn starch pudding, custard, etc. Makes two 9″ pies.

Raw Pudding

4 T. *alfalfa sprouts*
4 T. chopped dates or figs
1 organic apple, chopped, including *seeds*
1 organic fertile egg
8 ozs. raw milk (or yogurt)
2 t. raw *flax seeds*

In blender, add sprouts, fruit, and seeds. Blend at high speed. Set aside. Blend milk and egg. Warm slightly in saucepan. Pour in bowl with first mixture.

Plum Pudding Hard Sauce

1 C. raw butter
2 C. dark-brown sugar
1 T. vanilla extract
3 t. ground *plum kernels*
Cream (op.)

Cream butter and add sugar. Cream until smooth, then add kernels and extract. If necessary, a little cream may be added. Serves six.

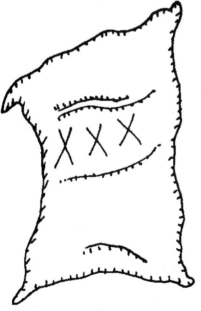

Almond Custard

4 C. milk (or home-made "imitation cream")
6 organic fertile eggs, beaten
6 T. **sorghum cane syrup**
2 t. **apricot kernels,** ground

Mix milk, eggs, and syrup well. Place in double boiler and cook over hot water (not boiling) until thick, stirring constantly. Serve over chilled berries. Serves four.

Sorghum Frosting

4 fertile egg whites, stiffly beaten
1 C. **sorghum cane syrup,** heated to simmer
¼ t. sea salt

Beat egg whites until very stiff. Slowly add the syrup while continuing to beat the eggs. Add the salt. Spread on yellow sponge cake.

Frozen Pudding Almond, Non-Dairy*

1 T. gelatin
2 T. cold water
⅓ C. boiling water
2 fertile eggs, separated
1 T. vanilla
½ C. raw honey
½ C. unrefined vegetable oil
½ C. almonds
2 t. ground **peach kernels** or **apricot kernels**

Soften gelatin in cold water in blender. Add boiling water and turn blender on high. Add the remaining ingredients, except the egg white. Set in refrigerator. When firm beat until creamy. Beat egg whites and fold in. Put in freezer tray and freeze until firm. Serve.

*This can be converted into non-dairy whipped cream by omitting the vanilla, honey, almonds, and peach kernels.

Carob Pot au Creme, Non-Dairy

6 oz. milk-free carob candy bar
¼ C. boiling water
6 eggs, fertile, separated
1 t. vanilla extract
2 t. *apricot kernels,* ground

Break up carob bar in blender. Add boiling water and blend at high speed until melted. Add the egg yolks and vanilla and blend again. Pour into a bowl. In a separate bowl, beat the egg whites until they stand in high peaks. Fold into the carob mixture and sprinkle the ground kernels on top. Chill until firm. Serves four.

Ozark Pudding

1 fertile egg
¾ C. dark-brown sugar
3 T. whole-wheat flour (or *buckwheat flour*)
1 T. active dry yeast, dissolved in ¼ C. very warm water
¼ t. sea salt
½ C. chopped raw walnuts
1 C. chopped green apples (Pippin or other)
1 T. vanilla extract
Seeds from the apples, ground

Mix all ingredients and place in 8″ pie dish. Let rise in warm place for about ½ hour. Bake for 35 minutes at 350° F. Serve with home-made vanilla ice cream or with "nutmeg" whipped cream.

Frozen Orange Cream, Non-Dairy

1 T. *flax seeds*
¾ C. water
3 fertile eggs, separated
⅓ C. honey, raw
3 T. almond oil
1 large can frozen
    unsweetened orange juice

Grind flax seeds to a powder in the blender. Add water and blend at high speed. Add remaining ingredients except the egg whites, and continue blending until smooth. Beat egg whites until they hold peaks. Fold in orange juice mixture. Pour into freezer tray and freeze.

Buckwheat Sweet Crumb Crust

3 C. *buckwheat flour*
2 small fertile eggs
⅔ C. soy or corn oil
½ t. sea salt
3 T. *sorghum cane syrup*
1 T. vanilla

Place flour in a bowl. Mix the eggs, oil, and remaining ingredients together and stir into the flour until crumbly. Press into pie plates and bake at 425° F. for about 20 minutes or until lightly browned. Fill with "Flummery" or "Raw Berry Pie" filling, etc. Makes two 9″ pies.

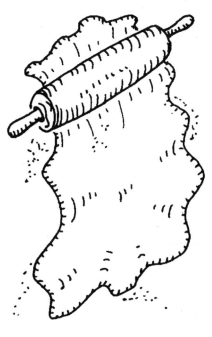

Pink Party Pudding

4¼ C. thinly sliced red apples
Seeds of the apples, ground
1 C. fresh *cranberries*
2⅓ C. raw honey
1 t. ground cinnamon
Pinch of sea salt
1½ T. arrowroot dissolved in
   ¼ C. cold water

Place all the ingredients, except arrowroot, in a covered saucepan and cook gently until fruit is tender. Add the arrowroot and stir until thick and clear. May be served with a whipped cream topping over whole-wheat cake or home-made ice cream. Serves four.

Almond Pastry Crust

1 cube raw butter
1 C. whole-wheat pastry flour
   (or rice flour)
¼ t. sea salt
½ C. ice water
1 fertile egg
1 t. *apricot kernels,* ground

Blend flour, butter, salt, and kernels together with your fingers or a pastry blender until the mixture has the texture of coarse corn meal with a few larger lumps of butter still present. Sprinkle a little ice water at a time, tossing mixed flour lightly to one side until the dough will hold together. Form into one large ball and one smaller ball. Roll out on pastry cloth. Gently settle into pie plate. Pour filling in and, making lattice with smaller ball, cover top. Beat egg and, with pastry brush, brush a little egg onto the pastry to give a golden glaze. The secret of a flaky crust is to keep the butter in the pastry very cold, so work quickly and don't let your warm fingers warm the butter. Bake in pre-heated oven with temperature given for the filling. Makes one crust with lattice top.

Cranberry Fruit Cake

3 T. active dry yeast
3 C. whole-wheat pastry flour
½ C. *buckwheat flour*
1½ t. sea salt
⅔ C. warm milk, raw
½ C. *sorghum cane syrup*
3 fertile eggs, beaten
2 t. ground *apricot kernels*
1¼ C. dates
1 C. *cranberries*
1 C. fresh pineapple, cooked
    down in ¼ C. wine for
    about 45 minutes
1½ t. ginger
1½ t. cinnamon
1 t. nutmeg

Mix 1 C. whole-wheat flour, salt, and yeast. Add the warm milk and syrup. Beat until smooth. Cover, place in warm area, and let rest for about 25 minutes. Stir butter, eggs, and kernels until creamy and beat into flour mixture. Beat in remaining flours, beating very hard until smooth. Fold in the remaining ingredients, except the glaze. Pour into a greased and floured 3-quart mold. Cover and let rise for about 1½ hours. Bake at 350° F. for 15 minutes; then at 300° F. for 30 minutes. Cool and top with cranberry glaze.*

Bavarian Cream Non-Dairy

2½ T. gelatin
1 C. very hot water
½ C. unrefined, bland oil
6 T. raw honey
2 t. *apricot kernels*
1 fertile egg, separated
1 t. vanilla

Place gelatin in blender. Add the water and blend until the gelatin is dissolved. Add all of the remaining ingredients, except the egg white. Beat egg white until very stiff. Fold it into the mixture and chill.

*Cranberry glaze: Mix 1 C. home-made cranberry sauce, 1 t. grated organic orange rind, 2 T. organic orange juice and enough non-fat, non-instant powdered milk to make a thick glaze. Serves eight.

Almond Pie Crust

2 C. whole-wheat pastry flour
1½ t. sea salt
½ C. unrefined oil
¼ C. cold raw milk
2 t. ground *apricot kernels*

Mix flour, apricot kernels, and salt in a bowl. Measure oil and milk into a cup and add all at once to the flour mixture. Stir lightly until blended. Form into a ball and divide in two. Flatten one ball at a time onto wax paper. Place second sheet on top and roll out to desired diameter. Place in pie plate and peel off the paper. Settle crust into pie plate. Bake at 475° F. for about 10 minutes or until brown. Very good for making raw berry pie. Makes two 9″ crusts.

Pineapple-Banana Pie Filling, Non-Dairy

3 C. cooked or canned pineapple juice
¼ C. corn starch
1 banana
2 C. crushed cooked or canned pineapple
3 fertile eggs, separated
1 t. sea salt
Juice of 1 organic lemon
2 t. ground *apricot kernels*
1 baked, sweet *buckwheat* crust
2 t. *sorghum cane syrup*
1 t. vanilla

Mix cornstarch with ½ C. cold juice. Heat remaining juice to simmer and add the cornstarch. Stir until smooth and thick. Add the crushed pineapple, egg yolks, salt, lemon juice, and ground apricot kernels. Stir thoroughly. Line bottom of baked pie crust with sliced banana. Pour filling in next. Beat egg whites until stiff and add 2 t. sorghum cane syrup, pinch of salt, and 1 t. vanilla. Beat again, then spread on top of the pie. Bake in 300° F. oven until meringue is golden brown. Serve hot or chill. Makes a 9″ pie.

Cranberry Plum Pudding

2 C. whole-wheat pastry flour (or *buckwheat flour*)
2 T. yeast dissolved in 6 T. very warm water
1 C. *sorghum cane syrup*
¾ C. grated raw potato
¾ C. grated raw carrot
1½ C. *cranberries*
1 C. raisins
1 C. dried *currants*
½ t. sea salt
1 t. each of the following: cinnamon, nutmeg, cloves
1 T. grated lemon or orange peel, organic

Mix all ingredients together. Pour into one quart steam pudding mold with cover. Let rise one hour. Cover and steam two hours or until done in water bath at same level as pudding. Serve with hard sauce (pg.179). Serves six.

Almond Cake (flourless and sugarless)

8 large fertile eggs, separated
1 C. ground almonds, raw
1 t. ground *apricot kernels*

Beat whites of eggs until stiff. Blend in yolks very carefully by folding with rubber spatula. Blend in the almonds and the kernels the same way. Bake at 300° F. (no hotter) for 45 minutes. Use greased tube pan.

Variation: ½ C. carob powder may also be folded in.

Frosting:
4 oz. carob candy bar (El Molino or other)
¼ C. sour cream

Melt carob bar carefully in top of double boiler. When it is soft, mix in sour cream. Spread on cake while still warm.

Spicy Frosting

½ C. raw butter
¼ C. **sorghum cane syrup**
¼ t. cinnamon
¼ t. nutmeg
¼ t. clove
½ C. sour cream or whipped cream, raw
½ C. chopped **cashews**

Cream the butter until soft and smooth. Blend in the sorghum. Add the spices, nuts, and blend into the sour cream or whipped cream. Chill. Serve as a topping for cakes, French toast, pancakes, and waffles.

Date Nut Frosting

1½ C. dark-brown sugar
3 T. **sorghum cane syrup**
¼ C. water
2 fertile egg whites
¼ t. sea salt
1 t. vanilla extract
¼ C. chopped **raw macadamia nuts**
10 soft dates, seeded and chopped

Place first five ingredients in top of a double boiler. Mix well. Heat water to a boil, beating constantly. Continue beating until mixture holds a peak. Fold in vanilla, dates, and nuts. Spread on cake.

Almond Honey Frosting

1¼ C. raw butter, salted
1¼ C. raw honey
1¼ C. soy powder (Fearn or other)
1 T. ground **apricot kernels**
Non-fat, non-instant powdered skim milk (op.)

Blend all ingredients together until smooth. Add a little non-fat, non-instant powdered skim milk if it's not quite thick enough. Enough to spread on 9″ x 14″ cake.

Carob Fudge Sauce, Non-Dairy

6 oz. milk-free carob bar
¼ C. home-made "imitation cream"
2 t. *apricot kernels,* ground
¼ t. peppermint extract (op.)

Melt carob candy in double boiler. Take off heat and stir in the remaining ingredients. Serve over cakes and puddings.

Almond Mousse

3 fertile egg yolks
¾ C. *sorghum molasses*
1 C. raw cream, whipped
3 egg whites, stiffly beaten
3 t. *apricot kernels*
10 almonds, raw, unblanched

Beat egg yolks and molasses together until thick and creamy. Fold in the whipped cream, then the beaten egg whites. Pour into 1½ quart mold and freeze. Unmold on glass serving dish. Garnish with almonds. Serves six.

"Plum-Nuts" Ice Cream, Non-Dairy

1 T. *flax seeds*
½ C. ground and cooked *millet* (see p. 112)
2 C. water
1 T. lecithin
½ C. ground raw almonds
2 t. *plum kernels,* ground (or *apricot kernels*)
1½ C. *sorghum cane syrup*
2 eggs, fertile
½ C. oil, such as soy or corn
2 C. fresh plums (may be frozen, unsweetened)

Grind flax. Add the water, millet, and remaining ingredients. Pour into ice cream carton or plastic container and freeze.

Blackberry Ice Cream, Non-Dairy

1 C. ground and cooked *buckwheat* (see p. 112)
1 T. *flax seeds*
1 T. lecithin granules or powder
1½ C. raw honey
2 fertile eggs
½ C. oil, such as soy or corn
2 C. *blackberries* (may be frozen, unsweetened)

Grind flax dry in blender. Add water and other ingredients. Pour into plastic container and freeze.

Almond Frosting

1½ C. honey or *sorghum cane syrup*
2 fertile egg whites
1 t. *apricot kernels*, ground
1 t. vanilla
1 t. lemon juice, organic

Place honey or syrup in a saucepan and boil to a temperature of 232° F. or until it spins a thread. Beat egg whites until they stand in peaks. Add syrup slowly, beating constantly. Add remaining ingredients and continue to beat until mixture is thick enough to spread. Spread on Almond White Cake. Top may be sprinkled with about ½ C. grated raw almonds. Enough to frost a 9″ tube cake.

Buttercup Frosting

2 C. honey
3 fertile egg yolks
¼ t. sea salt
1 t. *apricot kernels*, grated
1 T. organic lemon rind, grated
1 T. organic orange rind, grated
1 t. organic lemon juice

In a saucepan, boil the honey until it reaches a temperature of 250° F. or until a small amount forms a hard ball when dropped in a bowl of cold water. Beat egg yolks until thick and creamy. Slowly drizzle in the honey while continuing to beat the eggs. When thick and of spreading consistency, stir in the flavorings and frost yellow sponge cake. Enough for a 9″ tube cake.

Home-Made Ice Creams

1 C. raw honey
1 qt. certified raw whipping
    cream (or home-made
    "imitation cream")
1 T. vanilla extract
½ C. grated unsweetened
    coconut
2 t. grated *apricot kernels*
¼ C. shaved, unblanched,
    unroasted almonds

Blend first three ingredients in blender until smooth and creamy. This takes about 30 seconds. Stir in coconut, apricot kernels, and unroasted almonds. Pour into two ice cube trays and freeze in ice cube section of refrigerator. Be sure to turn down refrigerator to "low" if freezer and refrigerator are all one unit. Or pour into 1½ quart plastic container and put in deep freeze. Ice cream is ready in four hours. The honey keeps this ice cream smooth and free of ice crystals. Serves four.

Variations: Add 2 T. carob or 2 T. decaffeinated, instant coffee.

Use any unroasted nut (except peanuts) in place of the almonds.

Replace two cups of the cream with two cups of *blackberries, boysenberries, huckleberries, gooseberries, quince,* peaches,* plums,* apricots,* cherries, red *raspberries* or *black raspberries*.

*With these fruits, include a few of their de-pitted and ground *seeds*.

Yin Yang Wellness
12131 Westheimer, Unit F
Houston, TX 77077
281-558-8989

Candy

Candy can contribute to health without sacrificing taste and eye-appeal, but since concentrated sweets discourage the appetite for other foods, we recommend that these foods be kept to a minimum. Use sorghum molasses or honey in place of refined sugar. Serve candy substitutes as well. These foods are high in vegetable protein, vitamins, and minerals. They include dried

fruits, such as apricots, dates, raisins, apples, cherries, prunes, pea
and peaches. Included also are unsalted, raw nuts and see
popcorn, and soy nuts.

A delicious substitute for candy is "fruit leather." This is ma
by puréeing raw, fresh fruit in the blender. Pour it out in thin she
onto a cookie sheet lined with pliofilm or plastic wrap. Let it dry
for about three days in a slightly warm oven. Roll it up in its plas
film and store in a cool dry place. This may be frozen. Fruit leath
were made by our pioneer ancestors. They are easily transported
they are dry and not sticky. They require no refrigeration and they
satisfy a sweet tooth. They are an excellent survival food. Try pea
apricot, fig, or plum. Add several spoonfuls of ground apricot k
nels for added nutrition.

Turkish Paste Candy

⅓ C. cold water
2 T. gelatin
1½ t. ground *apricot kernels*
3 C. dark-brown sugar
Pinch sea salt
¼ C. apple juice, organic
Powdered milk to cover

Dissolve the gelatin in the cold water. Boil the sugar and water for 5 minutes. Add gelatin and simmer 20 minutes. Remove from heat, add apple juice and apricot kernels. Rinse a 9″ x 5″ x 3″ pan in cold water. Pour in the mixture. Let stand overnight in the refrigerator. Cut into cubes with a warm knife and roll in powdered milk. May be wrapped in wax paper. Keep in cool dry area.

Festive Winter Fruit Roll

¾ C. dried, unsulfured apricots
¾ C. dried, unsulfured raisins
¾ C. pitted dates
1 organic lemon
1 T. grated organic lemon peel
1 t. ground *apricot kernels*
1 C. finely ground nuts, raw

Put apricots, raisins, and dates through food chopper, using fine blade. Sprinkle with a little lemon juice for easier handling. Include peel and apricot kernels. Shape into balls and roll in raw nuts. Makes approx. one pound.

Marzipan

1¼ C. unblanched almonds, unroasted
2 t. grated **apricot kernels**
2¼ C. dark-brown sugar
3 small fertile egg whites

Grind almonds, kernels, and sugar in the blender until very fine. Blend in egg whites with fingers one at a time. Knead until smooth and plastic. May be pressed into molds or formed into roll, chilled, and sliced. 1½ cups.

Stuffed Dates

1 lb. dates
¼ C. raisins, ground
¼ C. ground almonds, raw
2 t. **apricot kernels,** ground
1 t. grated lemon rind, organic

Slit date and remove seed. Make paste of remaining ingredients. If too dry, add a few drops lemon juice. Place a little paste inside date and press closed again.

Candy "Frogs"

1 lb. carob candy bar (or milk-free carob bar)
1 C. puffed **millet cereal**
1 C. chopped raw nuts, almonds, pecans, walnuts, etc. (not peanuts)
1 t. raw cream (or yogurt)

Melt carob bar in top of double boiler. Mix in remaining ingredients. Drop by spoonful onto wax paper. Cool and serve. Store in cool area.

Stuffed Dried Figs

1½ lb. dried figs
¼ C. ground dates
¼ C. ground raisins
¼ C. ground pecans
2 t. grated lemon rind
Non-instant, non-fat powdered milk (op.)

Slit side of figs. Insert paste made of remaining ingredients. Press figs closed again. May be dusted with non-instant, non-fat powdered milk.

Raw Almond–Paste Candy I

2 C. unblanched, raw almonds
3 T. fresh organic lemon juice
2½ C. honey, raw, mild
2 t. *apricot kernels,* ground

Grind almonds very finely. Add juice. Boil honey until it registers 240° F. Add to ground almonds and lemon juice. Add apricot kernels. Mix well. When cooler, knead until smooth. Cool. Store in jar in refrigerator. Allow to "ripen" for about 1 week. Use in cakes, pies, cookies, and coffee cake. Or slice and eat as it is as candy.

Raw Almond–Paste Candy II

1 C. raw almond butter (Hain or other)
1 C. raw honey
1 T. ground *apricot kernels*
Enough non-instant, non-fat powdered milk to make a heavy paste. This will probably be between 1½ C. to 2 C. powdered milk
Grated raw coconut.

Mix almond butter and honey together. Add apricot kernels. Mix in powdered milk with hands to make a stiff dough. Form into balls and roll in the raw coconut. Serve. May be stored in the refrigerator or frozen.

Bibliography

Altman, Lawrence E.; N. Y. Times; September 10, 1972

Bellew, Bernard; *Diet Dynamics*; Sherbourne Press; Los Angeles; 1971

Bickel, Walter; *Hering's Dictionary of Classical and Modern Cookery;* Fachburg 63, Giessen, Germany; 1970

Binzel, M.D., Philip E.; *Alive and Well; One Doctor's Experience with Nutrition in the Treatment of Cancer Patients*; American Media, Westlake Village, CA, 1994

Carrol, Anstice, and Vona, Embree; *The Health Food Dictionary;* Prentice-Hall Inc.; Englewood Cliffs, N.J.; 1972

Erasmus, Udo; *Fats That Heal & Fats That Kill*; Alive Books, Burnaby, B.C., Canada, 1996

Foster, E. M. (Chairman), Committee On Food Protection; *Toxicants Occurring Naturally in Food;* (Nat'l. Acad. of Science, Wash., D.C.; 1973)

Graves, Lulu, and Taber, Clarence; *A Dictionary of Food and Nutrition;* F. A. Davis Co., Publ.; Phila. PA; 1938

Griffin, G. Edward; *World Without Cancer;* The Story of Vitamin B_{17}, American Media, Westlake Village, CA; Second Edition, 1997

Griffin, R.N., B.S., Patricia Irving and Richardson, M.D., John A.; *Laetrile Case Histories; The Richardson Cancer Clinic Experience*; American Media, Westlake Village, Second Edition, 2000

Hunter, Beatrice T.; *Consumer Beware,* Simon & Schuster, Rockefeller Center, N.Y.; 1971

Hunter, Beatrice Trum; *The Natural Foods Primer;* Simon and Schuster; N.Y.; 1972

Kingsbury, John M.; *Deadly Harvest;* Holt, Rinehart & Winston; N.Y.; 1965

Kittler, Glen; *Laetrile, The Control for Cancer;* Paperback Libr.; N.Y.; 1963

Krebs, Ernst; *The Laetrile/Nitrilosides in the Prevention and Control of Cancer;* The McNaughton Foundation; Cancer Book House; Los Angeles. Also memo to M.S. (John Beard Memorial Foundation, San Francisco, Sept. 16, 1972)

Lappé, Frances; *Diet For A Small Planet;* Ballentine Books; Inc.; N.Y.; 1972

Larson, Gena; *Is There An Anti-Cancer Food?;* Prevention Mag.; Apr., 1972

Liener, Irving; *The Toxic Constituents of Plant Food Stuffs;* Academic Press; N. Y. City; 1969

Medigar, Oliver P.; *Edible Wild Plants;* Collier Books; N. Y. City; 1972

Patti, Charles; *The Food Book,* Fleet Press Corp.; N. Y. City; 1973

Selsam, Millicent E.; *Plants That Heal;* William Morrow and Co.; N. Y.; 1959

Smith, Henry; *The Master Dictionary of Food and Cookery;* Practical Press, Ltd.; Salisbury Sq.; London, Eng.; 1965

Stang, Alan; *Laetrile;* American Opinion Mag.; January, 1974

Tighe, Eileen; *Woman's Day Encyclopedia of Cookery;* Fawcett Publications, Inc.; Vol. 1; Rockville, MA; 1966

Ward, Artema; *The Encyclopedia of Food;* Peter Smith Press; N. Y.; 1941

Watson, Betty; *The Language of Cookery;* World Publishing Co.; N.Y.; 1968

Wise, William H.; *The Wise Encyclopedia of Cookery;* Grosset and Dunlap; N.Y.; 1971

Appendix

Foods containing B_{17} (Nitrilosides)

Vitamin B_{17} appears in abundance in untamed nature. Because B_{17} is bitter to the taste, in man's attempt to improve tastes and flavors for his own pleasure, he has eliminated bitter substances like B_{17} by selection and cross-breeding. It can be stated as a general rule that many of the foods that have been domesticated still contain the vitamin B_{17} in that part not eaten by modern man, such as the seeds in apricots. Listed below is an evaluation of some of the more common foods. Keep in mind that these are averages only and that specimens vary widely depending on variety, locale, soil, and climate.

Fruits	Range*	Seeds	Range*
blackberry, domestic	low	apple seeds	high
blackberry, wild	high	apricot seed	high
boysenberry	med.	buckwheat	med.
choke cherry	high	cherry seed	high
wild crabapple	high	flax	med.
market cranberry	low	millet	med.
Swedish (lignon)		nectarine seed	high
cranberry	high	peach seed	high
currant	med.	pear seeds	high
elderberry	med. to high	plum seed	high
gooseberry	med.	prune seed	high
huckleberry	med.	squash seeds	med.
loganberry	med.	strawberries	med.
mulberry	med.		
quince	med.	**Beans**	**Range***
raspberry	med.	black	low
strawberries	med.	black-eyed peas: low to med.	

*Range:

High—above 500 mgs. nitriloside per 100 grams food
Medium—above 100 mgs. per 100 grams food
Low—below 100 mgs. per 100 grams food

Beans (continued)	Range
fava	high
garbanzo:	low to med.
green pea	low
kidney:	low to med.
lentils	med.
lima, U. S.	low
lima, Burma	med.
mung	med. to high
shell	low

Tubers	Range
cassava	high
sweet potato	low
yams	low

Nuts (all raw)	Range
bitter almond	high
cashew	low
macadamia:	med. to high

Sprouts	Range
alfalfa	med.
bamboo	high
fava	med.
garbanzo	med.
mung	med.

Leaves	Range
alfalfa	high
beet tops	low
eucalyptus	high
spinach	low
watercress	low

INDEX